Also By Allison DuBois

DON'T KISS THEM GOOD-BYE

WE ARE THEIR HEAVEN

WHAT THE DEAD CAN TEACH US ABOUT LIVING A BETTER LIFE

SECRETS

of the

MONARCH

Allison DuBois

A FIRESIDE BOOK

Published by Simon & Schuster

New York   London   Toronto   Sydney

Fireside
A Division of Simon & Schuster, Inc.
1230 Avenue of the Americas
New York, NY 10020

Fireside and colophon are registered trademarks of
Simon & Schuster, Inc.

Designed by Jan Pisciotta

Manufactured in the United States of America

ISBN-13: 978-0-7432-9114-9

Dedications are for people who impact your life in a profound way, so here goes:

To my girls, to whom I will pass a heavy torch. I know they will be great at whatever they choose to do in the world, and I will always love them, even when they make me mad. Just kidding, girls! I mean it, I always will love them.

To my husband, Joe, who puts up with my temper tantrums and holds me when the world is rough.

To my grandma Jenee, who taught me to "see outside the box." Of course to my parents, Mike and Tiena, who brought me into this world.

To the people of Pinetop who allow me to revisit my childhood whenever I go up there. It renews me, and I feel like I'm coming home.

Last but not least, to Steve Irwin, the Crocodile Hunter, who left a lasting impression on me and my family by allowing us to observe his truly remarkable existence. Our hearts go out to his family, who have shown us what grace, love, and dignity look like.

Contents

Foreword

*W*riters are a funny breed; they plan ahead and then they let the writing take them where it needs to go. If we consider inspiration to flow like water, writers are canal builders. Allison is no different. She has had the idea of this book for three years. She had this idea before the show *Medium* aired. She had this idea before her first book was published. I know this because I have the original unedited notes she made and they are dated. The original notes are from another point in our life and, as you will see, they have a different meaning now. This is a story of metamorphosis.

MONARCH

6-13-04

Dad, please play Circle of Life for Aurora's b-day today. I just need to know that today you're here with us.

Initially these notes were to become a chapter in Allison's first book. I do not know why she named this draft chapter "Monarch." I have asked her, and she tells me that it just sounded right. Since her first book was written soon after her father died, everything she wrote at the time was colored by the loss of her dad. In this case, she was reflecting on how she felt while celebrating our oldest daughter's birthday and yet still missing her father. I am always fascinated and amazed at how Allison's abilities permeate every element of her life. She does not have the luxury of having to imagine that her father could hear her. I say that it is a luxury to have to imagine the otherside because the person who "knows" that the otherside can hear her must then face the emotional consequences if the deceased does not respond.

Aurora was born when *The Lion King* came out and since then "Circle of Life" has been her song from us. It was my daughter's tenth birthday and I missed my dad. I was aware that you can't make demands on the otherside, but I wasn't making a demand—I was making a daughter's request from the heart. Maybe he would hear me. I then walked out the door with Joe and the kids to grab some breakfast. As we drove to McDonald's, I thought of how much my dad loved Aurora and how he would light up when he saw her. Today I was happy, happy to have daughters who are all in one way or another a reflection of my father.

The circle of life is a very inspirational concept. It can really help us put our own lives into perspective. It can help us see a bigger picture. It is a way to describe the monarch principle that Allison teaches about in this book. As I mentioned, Allison did not know why she titled this passage "Monarch"; she said it just sounded right. It was later, after I read her notes, that I told her that the monarch butterfly takes several generations to complete its journey north, only to turn around and fly back to where its great-grandparents came from. I believe that at that moment we began to realize the depth of this concept.

> I was in the kitchen with Joe, and I bolted up and ran to my room. "It's the song, my dad's playing the song!"
>
> My husband came trailing into our room.
>
> Joe said, "I'll get Aurora."
>
> As I wept, grateful that my father had acted so quickly, a picture popped into my head of my dad holding Aurora in the hospital when she was born. The words to the song were poignant and both soothed me and unraveled me simultaneously.

A great number of things came together at that moment. Aurora was born at a time that allowed this song to be special to us. Allison's ability and personality and heart had put her in a position to yearn for that song to be played. Allison's father had a heart big enough to make Allison's request a reality. The three generations were in that room on that day listening to a song that encapsulates a large part of the message Allison would eventually deliver in her third book, but the most profound statement was yet to be uttered.

Aurora came up to me and smiled.

"Aurora, Grandpa played this for you. It's your birthday present from him."

"I know, Mom."

She knows! Wow, my kids understand. That means everything to me.

This is really incredible. Aurora knew what was going on, she knew it was from Grandpa! It was very clear to me at that point that, like the butterfly and the circle of life, in our family each generation is passing on a gift to the next so that future generations can fly as high as and in any direction they desire.

Joe looked at me.

"Allison, you jumped up before the song ever came on the radio. You entered our room when the first couple notes began."

Yeah, I wasn't quite sure how I heard the radio

from across the house. I guess that's one of the benefits of doing what I do.

"Thank you, Daddy, for never leaving me."

I'm sharing this story with you because continuing communication after a death is so important because we remain connected. Tell your children about those important to you who have passed away. Let them know that we are not alone.

It was time to write her third book, and Allison was not sure which direction to go in. She had the original notes, but now they had a new meaning. Like the caterpillar's great metamorphosis into a butterfly, the original thought had changed into a different concept without losing its original meaning. The monarch concept is that our individual lives are part of a bigger story involving our friends and our family. I realized that the monarch's story is more than a beautiful example of a butterfly's metamorphosis; it is also the story of multiple generations building upon each other's work and energy, and most important, creating a circle of life, each of them relying on the others to do their part in order to place all of them where they belong in the grand scheme. My wish to you is that you be able to recognize the efforts of past generations and see the potential of future generations in your family, allowing you an overall view of the lessons there are both to learn from and teach to others. I've also learned from Allison that adopted people still belong to a tapestry of family; it's just a bigger tapestry, and they tend to be some of the most introspective people, listening for the inner voice of where they came from and where they want to go. This is a good trait.

Many people ask me how I do it, how do I live with Allison? At first this offended me. I would think, how could I *not* live with Allison? I married her because I could not imagine living without her. Then I came to realize that what people were trying to ask is how do you live with someone who can read your mind? I found my circle of life by answering this question for myself.

I see themes in my life. I am a product of my parents and grandparents. The little things and not so little things that I grew up with helped make me the person who is happily married to a medium.

Being married to a medium means that I must accept that people die. When people die, it is a very tragic event that affects many people and it is difficult for the survivors to get back to a normal life. Many people's reaction is to ignore death until it affects them directly because the emotions are so painful and it can be difficult to find the words to talk to someone who has lost a loved one. The thought of death often gives people the willies, probably because they consider their own demise. I am not different from other people; I just was fortunate to have a grandfather, Joe, who managed cemeteries for the Catholic church. This normalized death for me and made death a natural part of where I came from without emotionally devastating me. I thank my grandfather for this gift that he probably never knew he gave me nor knew how important it would be in my life. His wife, Marion, was sugar and spice and everything nice, and I always knew that I was loved.

Being married to Allison also means that I will continually have to learn about what she does and share what I have learned with others. My other grandparents, Paul and Mary, were teachers. Although I don't remember meeting my grandfather—he died when I was very young—I always seemed to feel that he was just around the corner, out of sight but close by. I always assumed this was because I was close to my grandmother, and she loved her husband very much. Now that I am older, I realize that although it is certainly the case that she loved him very much, there may have been more to my feelings. My grandmother was spry for her age and full of personality. She would pass on her knowledge in little tidbits like, "Live your life like it is on the front page of the paper." Little did I know that this would not be far from the truth.

I grew up the youngest of five boys in a stable

household. My father was a chemical engineer, and my mother, MaryFrances, was a teacher, although she stayed home to raise my brothers and me. My childhood taught me to be pragmatic and a critical thinker and to eat as fast as you can or your brothers will get all the good food. The common adage that it is better to beg forgiveness than to ask permission did not apply in my house. It was always better to be strong in who you are and accept the consequences; this would serve me well later.

As methodical and questioning as my father trained me to be, he also gave his life for me to accept what Allison does. My father died several months before I met Allison. She never met him in life. Allison and I dated for a year prior to our marriage. It was then several more years before she revealed to me that she could communicate with the dead. The very first people she brought through were my father and my grandfather. Her details regarding my father wearing bow ties and carrying a slide rule (he had a slide rule collection) were right on. She also said things about my grandfather that I didn't know until my aunt corroborated them, like that he loved and missed Boston clam chowder. I did not grow up in Boston, so I was not aware that there was a distinction between New England and Boston clam chowders.

People seem very interested in how I live with someone who can read my mind. Allison has been this way for as long as I know, so it is nothing new to our relationship. When I first met her, I fell in love. It did not seem so strange that this woman I fell in love with could finish my sentences and seemingly know my thoughts; isn't that all a part of being in love? It also makes me wonder how many little white lies and possibly bigger fibs other people are living with. Now, knowing that I grew up being taught to be who I am and to live like my life was on the front page, it is not hard for me to live with someone who can read my mind.

I think it really goes to show that Allison loves me. She has to accept and deal with me. I am an open book to her and she still loves me. The only difficulty is in exchanging presents. Lately I have taken a different tack and rather than trying to hide the present, I hype the present like a coming event so that she can get really excited about it!

Now, back to butterflies. A monarch butterfly can teach us to put our life in context with the lives of others around us. There is another butterfly effect that I learned about while studying nonlinear dynamics in my graduate-level mathematics classes. This butterfly effect is the root of chaos theory and was first articulated by Edward Lorenz. It refers to the characteristic of chaotic systems to have greatly varying final states due to subtle differences in initial conditions. In other words, a ripple effect that is often

Preface

I've titled my book *Secrets of the Monarch* having been inspired by monarch butterflies. I see a beauty in their families that also exists in ours. What I mean by this is that it takes monarch butterflies several generations to complete migration to secure the survival of their future families.

People are not so different; we spend a lifetime trying to learn lessons, become wiser, and pass this on to our kids and grandkids. We can't live forever, but a part of us will remain through memories of us and will continue to move our family and friends forward. Everyone has a path to walk that will help someone he or she loves to do more, be more, and learn more, so that person in turn can pass it on to future loved ones who will do the same, and so on. So pass on your family stories and traditions to others so they can live richer lives through your touch.

The purpose of my book is to help people live better lives and to realize how precious being alive is so that they savor their days as they move through life. Part of appreciating depends upon connecting with other people and learning their stories. Through this process you become a stronger empathic as well as a great student of life. Remember, if you live well, you will die without regrets, and that is the key to being true to oneself and those we love. This is not achieved through selfishness or greed but rather through empathy, wisdom and, often, assertiveness.

Secrets of the Monarch

CHAPTER 1

Leaps of Faith

I wrote this chapter not only to share with you my own experiences but also to acknowledge that believing in life after death can be a leap of faith for many. We have faith in people we love—our kids, spouse, friends. When they die, why would we not believe that they continue to deserve our faith? Anything that you invest your heart in is a leap of faith that opens you up to potential pain. But without that leap, so much would never be seen or felt by us. Follow me through this chapter as I try to show you life through my eyes so that you can take a second look at your own.

In May of 2006 I was on a book tour for my second book, *We Are Their Heaven*. One of my stops was in beautiful Denver, Colorado. It was picturesque and the people were salt of the earth. I was booked on a morning TV show called *Colorado and Company*. My "host" (aka "babysitter," who's hired so that I don't miss an interview) and I walked into the green room to wait for our segment of the show to be filmed. I noticed that a petite, well-dressed woman had turned my way. She was refined yet approachable and immediately friendly. We introduced ourselves, and that moment would start a relationship that would leave a lasting impression on countless lives—including yours, I hope.

The lady before me was Frances Owens, the first lady of Colorado. She complimented me, saying that she was a fan of the show *Medium* that's inspired by my own life story. I was introduced to two other women who were on the set to be interviewed for the show as well. They help run the Heart Light Foundation that helps grieving families through counseling and resources in their time of need. They were trying to convince me to come back to Denver and speak to their bereavement group. At the time I had a hectic schedule and it was hard to imagine a return anytime soon. I thanked them and took the stage where Denise and Mark were waiting to interview me. They are two of my favorite morning show hosts, by the way. They are excellent when it comes to motivating you to deliver a good interview by prodding you with their great senses of humor. I left Denver impressed by the people and very fond of the city.

The Heart Light Foundation contacted my husband, Joe, along with Frances Owens and started the momentum that would inevitably return me to Denver in five months. Our little girls had just changed schools and decided they were not going to leave their new friends so quickly, so Joe and I headed off to Denver, just the two of us. It was late on October 19, 2006, and Joe and I were relaxing over dinner at the Keg Steakhouse. Our server's name was Devlin, and Joe and I proved irritating by throwing in some of our own kindergarten plays on his name. He was a great sport, though, and humored us. The table next to us had a couple who were really good at making sucky noises with uncomfortably long kisses, which prompted Joe and me to exit for a good night's sleep. I know you know what I'm talking about, as we have all had neighbors in a restaurant who warranted a replay of their actions to our friends.

The next morning it was back to *Colorado and Company*, where this time I was on with comedian Hal Sparks. He was fantastically funny as well as very nice, and he was promoting a show called the *Celebrity Paranormal Project* on VH-1. So I guess it's easy to see why he and I were booked on the same program.

Later that day I was off to the governor's mansion, where the lovely and gracious Frances Owens hosted a luncheon for me and I was able to meet with some of the people involved with the Heart Light Foundation. It was a wonderful, cool afternoon, and the company couldn't have been better. As I ate my cherry cobbler and tended to my usual allergy attack (I'm allergic to nearly every plant that grows), I could feel the traumatic loss of loved ones around some of the guests at my table. But it wasn't the time or the place for readings, so I pulled back on my natural instinct to "read" people and happily posed for pictures with the luncheon guests.

When it was time to go, I loaded up the car with Joe and my friend Andrea, who's from Colorado and was nice enough to come have lunch with us that day. It was a long day and it wasn't over yet; I had three hours to kill until the book signing and speaking engagement for the foundation.

On our way to the event, it started to rain, making it difficult to read the sign on the door we had been sent to. After close inspection, we saw that the sign was directing everyone to a different building, so we shuffled back into the car and made our way across the dark parking lot. Upon entering the building, I was intercepted by foundation members and taken into a side room. As I sat talking to Andrea, I realized I couldn't breathe. I shared this with the ladies in the room, and they apologized and explained to me that this room was used for viewings at funerals. Yep, you guessed it, my signing had been set up in a funeral parlor. Not good! I had never conducted an event in a funeral home and I never intended to. As a matter of fact, I hadn't been back to a funeral home since my own dad had died, and this was not easy for me. I quickly made my way out of the viewing room into the entrance and took a very long breath of fresh air as I processed the enormity of the moment and realized what I had to do whether it was difficult or not.

I was led to an open door where Joe and Andrea waited with me until I was announced to the crowd. I leaned up against the wall in the hallway as my eyes fell on a corner filled with children's toys. I could visualize the kids who had sat there playing with the toys. These kids were not like other kids. They didn't play with toys in a carefree manner out of enjoyment. These kids were overwhelmed with death in the family and played with the toys as a distraction, a sort of lifeline, if you will. The toys served as their only line of defense on a day when they would be invisible to the adults around them.

My heart broke for the children who played in sorrow as their mother, father, sibling, or grandparent was being mourned in the other room. Playing with a race car or blocks as they absorbed the pain of the day exuded by the mourners. They are little conduits designed to "feel" for others, which makes them so special and vulnerable. I snapped back to the moment as I heard my name announced. I attempted to clear my head through a deep breath and a quick prayer.

As I walked through the doorway and around the corner, my eyes grew wide as I took in my audience seated in pews in the actual funeral parlor. It resonated in my heart that these same people had sat in these same pews when they attended the actual funerals of their loved ones. The same loved ones whom they had hoped to experience on the night of my book signing. I'm usually composed, but I had had a feeling ahead of time that this event was going to be emotionally taxing. Still, I was unprepared to feel the level of anguish that was quickly enveloping me. I looked to Joe for support, which he attempted to give me with an understanding glance.

Sometimes when I speak, I know that the words that come out of my mouth are being directed to someone specific in the crowd who was intended to receive and be touched by the words. This night was no exception.

After my emotional speech and scanning every tearful face in the crowd, I settled myself at the signing table in the front entrance. I instantly felt relieved of the weight on my chest that held me back from both breathing and sobbing. The audience formed a lengthy line, and I hesitantly and slowly took in the crowd. I drew them in with my eyes and my breath. The people were well-groomed and full of great character. I connected with them one by one.

One young woman thanked me for being there, and it turned out our dads had died the same week of the same cause and shared similar personality traits. This meant a lot to me since I was contemplating the fact that I hadn't seen my own father in quite some time. The sad yet pretty blonde wept with a smile of understanding, realizing I was not so different from her. Seeing that our pain was the same reminded us both that we weren't alone and created a camaraderie between us. I shook her hand and wished her well.

I looked at the next person in line, a very tall man proudly wearing a gold chain around his neck with a ring hanging from it. I said, "Oh, you wear your dad's ring too." He looked at his wife and said, "Did you hear that?" She nodded in acknowledgment. His dad had been very good-looking and all that the son had measured himself by. The man in line was a really special guy in his forties who shared his dad's good looks.

I smiled and thought of the power that our dads had passed on to us. They owned our hearts and we owned theirs. I also believe that they gave us backbone to stand up with complete certainty and the courage that would be required to walk in their deep footsteps. Without their request or expectation, we had "it," whatever "it" was. Our dad's approval and love are unique and significant, and unlike other's because a dad plays such an important role in our lives. We don't know why we need his approval, we just know that part of us requires it. The satisfied man walked out the door with all that he needed, and I understood his childlike acceptance of the moment expressed through the big grin on his face and the gleam in his eyes. I emotionally tipped my hat to him.

Next in line was a young woman who held an infant son in her arms. Any woman would be rendered helpless by the organic light in the little boy's eyes. The young woman's energy was like that of any friend in our youth whom we had ever valued but lost track of, and in retrospect realized that she had been too quickly dismissed. Her friend introduced herself to me, and I instantly thought that both were women I could be good friends with. I could see the loss worn on their faces and I could clearly see their excitement to be there, as well as how nervous they both appeared.

There is always an expectation that I feel when I sign a book to "right a wrong," which I know I can't always do because it's not always in my court to do so. I do, however, have a habit of signing some books with the words from the headstone of the deceased. I looked at the young mom and her son as well as her friend. I looked down at my book; I stared at the cover that read, *We Are Their Heaven*. I remembered the moment that those words first left my lips years ago. I opened the book to the title page, again staring at those important words. I wrote, "She Walks With Angels." The sister of the deceased ran out of the building with her son in her arms. Her friend said, "It's okay, those are the words on her sister's headstone. Her sister was also my best friend. She just wasn't expecting that. I'll be right back."

I pleadingly looked at my friend Andrea as I watched a heavy tear roll down her flushed face.

"Andrea, I'm sorry, you haven't seen firsthand what I do before. I should have prepared you." As I bowed my head in apology, she gripped my hand and said, "Allison, I'm crying for you. I had no idea what your life really was. I'm so sorry."

"Andrea, don't feel bad for me. I get to see what many can't. Don't ever feel sorry for me. I'm lucky. Sometimes I am wrenched inside when someone can't see what I can or hear what I do, but I just wish everyone could see them like I do, that's all. I'm happy to be who I am and I'm used to freaking people out. The beauty is that what I wrote in her book will mean something to her and her family for the rest of their lives. How great is that?"

She shot me a sympathetic smile and a wink of friendship. You have to understand that Andrea is the equivalent of sugar and spice and everything nicer than we are. You've got to love her!

I have many friends who do what I do in one form or another. They put bad guys away and have to live with their "heroic" existence, not because they tried to be heroes but because they were born to be. They never will see themselves as that, though, and that's part of why they're so great. They're profilers, cops, district attorneys, judges, medical examiners, and law enforcement agents all deserving of the title hero, but they're humble, which makes them even more deserving of the position.

On the flip side, and hear me on this, some people who walk the earth can make angels look dirty because they are so good. We're created with reminders that we can always be better. Heroes give us that contrast, and so do people like Andrea who "feel" for others with their whole heart. I bet most people have crossed paths with a person capable of casting a shadow on an angel, and angels would call them friends.

The young woman who ran from the building earlier walked up to me with her baby and apologized for racing off. I hugged her and told her there was no need for that. As I stood with one arm around the young woman, her baby, and her friend, I knew that her deceased sister was locked arm in arm with us. We smiled for the camera, *all* of us. I looked at the baby and he stopped fussing and smiled as he grabbed for me. His mom commented that he doesn't usually want to go to someone other than her. I grinned at him and said, "You can see them in my eyes and I can see them in yours." He laughed and we parted ways after an unforgettable moment. I connected with hundreds of people that night, and even through the sorrow we all walked out of the event feeling blessed beyond words.

HANGMAN

Joe and I took our girls and headed up to Pinetop, Arizona, to our vacation home. I was ready to get out of the city, away from the monotony and crime. We had just entered the outskirts of town when we saw a trading post, and after a little begging from my girls I relented and we stopped. Entering the store, our family was greeted by a genuinely nice man who ran the store. Our girls ran about picking up stones out of the many baskets that held them: alum, amethyst, fool's gold. They were beautifully colored and sparkling, and my girls wanted them all. They each settled on two and I began making my own way through the many treasures in the store. My girls aren't the only ones in our family who like to shop.

A case full of old photographs caught my eye; I do

love old pictures. Upon inspection, I noticed a photograph from Texas dated 1880. In the photograph were five men who had been hanged. The details of their faces were visible, and in the background you could see the horse whose back they had been seated on just before their demise. I was a little shocked to see the picture that had been taken 126 years earlier in a frame on display in a little shop in Arizona. After we left the store, I couldn't get the image of the men out of my mind. My girls were buzzing with joy over their new finds and Joe had tunnel vision intent on getting to our cabin. We had a wonderful getaway, and after a couple of days we headed back to our home in the city.

A few weeks passed and I decided to go up to the cabin again with my friend Wendy for the fourth anniversary of my dad's death. I wanted to clear my head and think of my dad and all the good times that we'd had. This included but was not limited to all of the movies that we saw together while I was growing up. We laughed over *Stir Crazy,* cried over *E.T.,* screamed together while watching *Invasion of the Body Snatchers,* and played movie trivia for years. We had so many good times together; he was fun with a capital *F.* We even were known to have an occasional popcorn fight as we tried to catch stray puffs in our mouth. These were the memories that I needed to hold on to and reflect on at my cabin.

Wendy and I started out on our road trip playing great tunes from the seventies and swilling soda. Sometimes it's nice to have a girls' road trip; it makes you realize how lucky women are to be moms, sisters, and daughters. Along the way, I told Wendy about the picture of the men who were hanged and that I could not get it out of my head.

"Wendy, I think I should buy the photograph."

"Why?"

"Because I think I should burn it. I have a feeling that not all of those men were guilty. Aside from that, those men have been captured in death for over one hundred years as they hung from nooses. Pictures carry energy, and even if they've moved on they can never fully let go of their moment of death because so many still see it. Does that make sense to you?"

Wendy mulled over the thought and replied with, "Yeah, I think you should do it!"

Now we were two women on a mission. As soon as we entered town I said, "There, that's the trading post."

Wendy's eyes gleamed with anticipation, as did mine. What would I say to the cashier when I purchase this morbid picture? Why did I care? My mind was racing with possible scenarios and random thoughts.

Wendy was busy poring over the many types of sage you can burn to clear a house of any difficult energies. I nervously motioned to the cashier to come over with a key to open the case.

"Which one do you want, honey?" she asked.

"Uh, that one." I pointed to the black-and-white photo of misery. I felt like I owed her some sort of explanation, so I blurted out, "I'm a history buff," which is true, "and that time period is especially interesting to me."

She seemed content with my answer and rang up my purchase. I practically ran to my car with Wendy, hurrying past the tepees and boxes of rusty horseshoes.

"Now what?" Wendy inquired.

"Well, let's drop off our luggage at the cabin. I'm not burning the photo there, just in case the deceased men decide to hang out in some sort of appreciation."

"Good thinking, Allison."

We unloaded our luggage and I took emotional inventory of myself knowing that today was the anniversary of my dad's death. Yep, this was a hell of a distraction, I thought.

I then heard an old Roger Miller song playing in my head, "Please release me, set me free . . ." The song was drowning out my ability to hear myself think; it kept playing over and over again in my head. I was somewhat familiar with the song from all those years of playing name that tune with my dad. He liked the oldies, so I knew the lyrics pretty well and I knew that all of the lyrics didn't apply to the situation, but I understood the gist of the message.

The moment in time that the photograph had captured held the men's shame. It needed to go, and they were urging me to make this happen. The men in the picture were not proud of the moments that led up to the picture; they regretted their actions, and I feel that at least one of the men was in the wrong place at the wrong time and had no responsibility for the crimes. The men had paid for their crimes with the loss of their lives, plus they had been sentenced through that photograph to over one hundred years of the shame of being gawked at and reduced to a souvenir in a trading post. The men had paid a painfully high price, and their sentence was about to come to an end.

"Where to, Allison?"

"I know exactly where, Wendy, the Lion's Den. It's the town watering hole, and it's very western and rugged with true Arizona charm. It has the modern-day cowboys who drive pickup trucks and Harley-Davidson motorcycles. There's an outdoor area outside of the tavern that's perfect. I bet the deceased men would feel at home there, and it's outside so they won't be emotionally tied to the building. Besides, it's already haunted! I'm sure they won't hang out, I'm just hedging my bets."

Wendy and I arrived at the Lion's Den, and I ordered a round of drinks to make a toast to my dad. She waited at the table as I walked through the building to the courtyard area with the picture in my hand. I walked to the end of the yard and took a seat on a wooden bench. I held the picture in one hand and a lighter in the other. I then carefully lit a corner of the picture that for 126 years had existed, since the day those men drew their last breath. The camera that produced the picture was long gone. This picture had made its way from Texas to a small town in Arizona. Somehow all these years later it had caught my eye and had brought me to this moment when it was about to perish forever. As I watched the picture burn, I knew that this was no coincidence. The old photo didn't burn easily, and it took a lot of relighting to remove the men's images, but I made sure the faces were no longer visible beneath the nooses. I felt relief wash over me, and the atmosphere instantly felt lighter. I took a deep, cleansing breath and said, "There you go. It's up to you now to right your wrongs."

I'm not a big supporter of many spirits being bound to earth because of bad things. When they do remain, it's usually because they feel emotionally connected to a building or person because they feel good when they're around them rather than bad. There are exceptions to this, of course, and in the case of the men who were hanged, it's not that they were bound to the photo's setting but rather that they were tugged at every time someone looked at the picture of their shame. They were capable of moving on, but there's a power that allows the living to connect to the dead through pictures and memories.

When we think of our loved ones who've passed, they feel pulled toward us and they reminisce with us as we pour over memories of them and pictures of happy times. For the deceased men in the picture it's no different, except they don't have people looking at their pictures to reminisce over happy memories with them. The people who looked at their picture were strangers looking at potential souvenirs, so the connection was not healthy or good for anyone.

Can I scientifically prove that my burning the picture made a difference? No. Do I need that information to know that my actions made a difference? No. I hope that as people evolve spiritually, they recognize that you don't need other people's approval to validate your senses or feelings throughout life. Is it a leap of faith in yourself? Yes. Is faith in yourself a wise investment? Yes, definitely.

The rest of that night was devoted to the memory of my father. It was the first time since his death four years prior that September 22 was a day that was filled not with tears but instead with a whole lot of life. That day would be the first of a string of spiritual events that would take place for me in Pinetop. The town has history and it was quickly becoming an important part of mine.

In December of 2006, my family and I returned to Pinetop for a little rest and relaxation at the cabin we lovingly call "The Lazy SOB." For those with a sense of humor, this is a great name for a cabin. Work with me now. Joe and I watched our one-year-old pug Eleanor attempt to eat all of the snow on the sledding hill and it ended in a draw between our dog and the mountain. I mentioned to Joe that a trip to the Lion's Den was in order, not just because the people are friendly but also because I had heard that the basement was particularly haunted, and I wanted to see for myself. Understand that a trip to a haunted location is like a trip to an amusement park for me.

When I walked into the saloon I asked for the owner, George. He's a real doll and I wanted a tour of the basement. George approached me with a warm smile. I gave him my request and he obliged with a puzzled glance. Probably because I was smiling and "at home" and a little too excited to tour a haunted basement. Before he opened the door, I asked him, "Is there an escape door out of the basement?" I had been told of one that morning by a calm voice as I dried my hair in the bathroom.

When I hear information like that and it's not public knowledge, it's important for me to verify my information for my own personal record of my consistency and accuracy. George walked me over to a door that passes from the basement to outside the building. I was pleased. I then walked around the basement, aware that what surrounded me were indeed the walls of a haunted building, and something or someone lay in wait for company. George says he leaves Christmas lights on in the basement so that it's always lit because it's a little frightening down there. It didn't feel like the spirits were harmful in any way, just "fond" of the bar.

I looked at George and told him that a man had been killed in the basement during a card game gone wrong. He wasn't sure of that, so he asked a woman named Jody who just happened to be there that day to verify the information. She nodded and said that sounded very similar to a story that she heard from a man I'll call Sam who was a native of the area and who had heard all the stories about the Lion's Den when he was growing up.

There was an area that people are afraid to go to in the basement, but I felt drawn to it. George's eyes widened and he shared that maybe that wasn't a good place for me to be. I, on the other hand, was ready to take a shovel to the ground to look for artifacts. I know that sounds a little out there, but for a medium, being in a treasure trove of spirits like that is exhilarating. I told George I saw a baby being born down there in the past to a man that was dark skinned and a woman who had lighter skin. He shared that the original owner, Walsh Mac, was a black man that opened the bar because he wasn't allowed into other bars because of his color. I'm sure Walsh made a big difference in the lives of many of his patrons and employees who shared his same plight. Walsh sounded like a maverick to me, and I immediately liked him. He definitely had racial obstacles in the early twentieth century, but he persevered.

George also shared that there had been a house of prostitution a stone's throw from there. It's not far-fetched to think that one of the prostitutes might have given birth there from any one of various potential fathers. A local was able to confirm that a baby had been born down in the basement, which reinforced my vision. Joe took a picture of the basement, and there was a very obvious orb present. It was perfectly round and white, and there were no others visible. I don't care what "professional" skeptics think, I believe that a spirit's energy can be captured on film.

The Lion's Den still has the feel of the saloon that it was in the early twentieth century, and the staff say they've had many run-ins there with those who've preceded us in death. They say if you clink your glass twice and toast Walsh Mac, you'll feel him around you. Joe and I raised our glasses to Walsh, and if I've ever seen Joe turn white it was when he felt a hand grab his shoulder from behind. I loved it because there was no one visibly there!

George has had this same experience there, and it couldn't be more real if it was a living person standing behind you. Similar human energies (people) are drawn to the same kind of places, so wouldn't it make sense that spirits would be drawn to the living who remind them of themselves, others who feel familiar and welcoming? If you are a sarcastic person with a dry sense of humor, then you tend to draw that same energy to you, which is why we can see a piece of ourselves represented in each of our friends. If you look around, you'll truly recognize a character trait of yours good or bad reflected in your friends. This applies to the living and the dead—if there's a similar energy, we will gravitate to it.

Many people ask, "Why do spirits linger in old buildings?" It varies from individual to individual, but the reasons tend to be similar. I'll use Mac as an example. There's an obvious reason why Walsh Mac remains around the Lion's Den: The people who patronize his old bar like to cut loose and listen to good music just like he does. There's a high energy level created by dancing, laughter, and music, and this includes spirits.

Souls are made of energy, and energy can be attracted by similar frequencies to its own. From what I've experienced, criminals have a frightening energy that "feels" dangerous; drug addicts have a low energy that "feels" like a chemical imbalance but one that they helped create; humanitarians carry a nurturing "feeling" that feels safe. Mac likes footloose people, and they carry an energy that feels like it could lift you off the ground because it exists to raise your "spirit," so to speak; it's fun.

Pay attention to the energies around you that are living and see if you can get a "feel" for each one and learn to identify it in other people. Once you fine-tune your own sixth sense, you can take it a step further and attempt to identify those same energies among the dead. When I bring a spirit through who was a drug addict in life, I'm able to identify it because I've been around that same energy among the living and it's recognizable. Most people always have a pretty good sense of when someone "creepy" is around them because we pick up on this when we're kids and are still "sensitive." It's our first energy lesson in learning the difference between a good or bad energy that has entered our personal space. When you're energetically "repelled" by a person without his or her actions causing your reaction, it's an "energy" thing and should be recognized and respected. In other words, you just got a bad "vibe" from him even though he didn't actually do anything to you.

The more you practice, the better you get. Just remember to not second-guess your instincts after you've achieved a feeling of certainty. Otherwise you can be convinced that your feeling is wrong and then it doesn't do you any good.

Mac also was known to have spent many of his good days on that land and emotionally invested himself in the bar as he fought the battle against discrimination. People burned down his establishment, but he remained out of principle. Walsh hangs out at the Lion's Den for all of these reasons, and if you're ever in Pinetop, Arizona, and find yourself in the Lion's Den, make sure that you clink your glass twice for Walsh Mac. He might return the friendly gesture.

As a footnote, a few months after going down to the basement at the Lion's Den, I returned for a little bit of fun. There hadn't been a poker game played in the basement of the Lion's Den since the 1940s, so I thought it was time to fix that. I talked to George about setting up a game and he agreed that it might be fun. So it was on, a good old-fashioned smack down of cards.

(Now, everyone assumes that because I can predict things and pick up on people's thoughts, I win all the card games with unfair advantages. Let me state for the record that it is true that I know when to fold because I can "feel" if someone has a better hand or is bluffing, but my excitement can get the better of me and I stop paying attention to my "sense" and get caught up in the moment running on pure adrenaline. I also love to raise the stakes and I have been known to get carried away, so if you ever play cards with me, don't be too concerned about my abilities. I am a decent card player, though, so my skills are another story.)

Anyway, I tucked my jeans into my turquoise cowboy boots and took off through the snow for the game in the haunted basement. At the Lion's Den, I was greeted by George, who was sporting his big black cowboy hat on top of his sterling silver hair and looked ready to play. We walked down the creaky stairs and I saw that a frantic card game was already in progress. I found it exhilarating just to see a current card game being played down there instead of the traces of past games—the first real card game to be played down there in sixty years! I pulled up a chair. The cold was almost too much to bear, but the moment was so significant that I didn't care if I froze. I noticed that most of the Christmas lights that George left up year-round had burned out, and when I pointed this out to him he looked a little worried. I was introduced to the gang that had lived such interesting lives that most had a nickname to prove it. These guys had definitely played more card hands than I had. George introduced me to "Buckwheat" first, and I didn't ask him the story behind his nickname. All I knew was that he was very white skinned, so I spent the evening referring to him as "Cream of Wheat." Then I met "Speed Bump." I think he's called that because he plays a mean game of cards and he can slow you down pretty fast. I'm piecing this together from comments that the guys made to him during the game. Then there was "Detour," who was a kick in the pants. Nobody else had a nickname, so I'll leave it at that.

I was given my little plastic chips and I got a thrill out of watching the guys look somewhat nervous being down there. I couldn't talk any of them into crawling to the back of the basement where the ceiling gets very low to the ground. I listened to their stories of when a horse many moons ago had fallen through the floor and died in the basement. They also talked about the old playing cards they had dug up from the dirt. You have to understand how much I love hearing the history of buildings, especially ones that have great stories, like the Lion's Den.

After about twenty minutes, the guys had enough of the freezing cold and opted to move the game upstairs where there was heat. As I followed them up, I tried to convince them to get a shovel and go digging with me in the basement, but they weren't as keen on the idea as I was. So we played cards for about three hours, and I was ready to call it a night.

A very nice photographer had taken some great

snapshots. The photos were fascinating because they had a very clear mist that swirled into some interesting shapes, and in a couple of the pictures you could see detailed faces in the mist that were not ours. The faces looked to be male, which made sense since it was no doubt men who were dealing the cards and drinking the whiskey back in the day. I'm sure the cardplayers from the twenties, thirties, and forties were delighted to see a card game take place in the basement. After sixty years, I'm sure they thought it was long overdue. I'm sure the stories they told one another all those years ago as they drank whiskey and played cards would burn our ears.

Later that night, when the bar manager was closing up and putting up the bar stools, he apparently had the tar scared out of him by presences that were making it clear to him they were very much still there. George chuckled when he shared that with me, but he was adamant. "Allison, I'm serious, there was really something there."

I said, "George, I'm one of those people you don't have to convince. I believe you."

I'm always telling people to live life large and not to apologize for who you are. My participation in that card game in the basement that dark, snowy night will go down as one of my favorite experiences ever, all because I took a chance and asked George to make it happen. If I hadn't done that I'd never have known that special night, and I think people need to think more about what they miss out on because they're afraid to ask for what they want out of life. Take a chance and make your time here memorable. Remember, taking risks is what legends are made of.

CHAPTER 2

City Under Siege

In the summer of 2006 I was faced with a case like none I'd ever worked before. As long as we live there is always room to learn from circumstances unlike any we've ever known. None of us can ever have all the answers, only snippets of what we've seen and know to be true.

Phoenix was a city under siege from two separate killers who had made our streets their own personal killing fields. The first killer had started out with a string of robberies and sexual assaults, ultimately leading to homicides that all took place between August 6, 2005, and June 29, 2006. The toll of victims is thought to be somewhere around twenty. If this wasn't bad enough, another serial killer was running the streets randomly shooting his victims, both domestic animals and people. The police believe that this shooter started his crime spree on May 24, 2005, and ended it July 8, 2006.

This had never happened before in Arizona history. There was a question of whether the two killers might be connected. My hometown was in a state of panic as two serial killers ran the streets at the same time. One was dubbed the "Baseline Rapist/Killer" and the other was the "Serial Shooter." Both were deadly.

In July of 2006 I was on vacation on the East Coast visiting our friends the Grammers for the Fourth of July, which is also my youngest daughter's birthday. Unfortunately, of all the memories that I could take away with me, the one that sticks out the most prominently is watching TV with Kelsey and Camille and seeing the national news footage of the killings in Phoenix that were rising as quickly as our desert temperatures. I'll never forget the anger I felt knowing that the home I grew up in was under attack. It was unbearable.

I returned to Phoenix a couple of days later. Our plane landed at Sky Harbor and an eerie feeling came over me as I absorbed the heavy cloud that hung over our beautiful city. Since we were in our monsoon season, it was hot and humid outside, and fear permeated the air. I knew that this would be a touchy subject with the police, and I understood why they didn't want media connected to me tied into their cases; It's one of the downsides of being a public figure. I was also quite certain that I had to do something to help, though I wasn't sure what. I knew that working two cases at the same time could cause me to overlap their information, but that didn't change the fact that I had no choice but to try.

I consented to only three interviews concerning these cases to make sure that it didn't turn into a media circus focused on me instead of the crimes themselves. I also made an agreement with certain law enforcement members that I "would not confirm nor deny working with them," and that suited me fine. Again, "I cannot confirm nor deny that." There, I said it!

I wrote down the first name of all the victims and started writing down the impressions that I got connected to them. If they recognized the killer, I would feel a sense of calm. If I felt a sense of panic come over me, I didn't feel they knew him. Also, I can sense where a killer's anger stems from, and I felt that the Baseline Killer carried his anger from his family upbringing. Sometimes I'll "see" a name connected to the killer or "feel" why the killer targets people in certain areas.

In the summer of 2006, I consented to a TV interview with Pat McMahon, a trusted friend of mine. He loves Phoenix as much as I do, so much that I have nicknamed him "Mr. Phoenix." He's been a well-respected voice on TV and radio there for forty-plus years and he used to be on *The Wallace and Ladmo Show,* my favorite when I was a little girl. Knowing that I could trust him was key, since he'd make sure that the interview stayed productive and didn't become exploitative.

I had a raging cold that day, but I wanted to get the public to take a look at their neighbors and picture the perpetrator looking different from the police sketch since he had altered his appearance. For instance, he didn't have long hair like the sketch, kind of an important factor. The police had suspected that he might be disguising himself with wigs and other accessories. I could "sense" his length of hair as though it were on my head. I know, creepy! Also, he could pass for different ethnic backgrounds, so I advised people to keep an open mind when looking at their neighbors. His features didn't "feel" defined— they weren't clearly tied to one ethnicity or another— and the hue of his skin looked ambiguous. Yes, he was a minority, but he could pass for a few different ethnic backgrounds; he wasn't particularly dark and he wasn't white. He was exactly somewhere in between.

So with dreams of taking a Benadryl to stop up my sinuses, I took the platform with Kleenex in hand, not a good look for me. I gave the motives for the killers as I saw them and descriptions of their personalities, and I said that I did not believe that the Baseline Killer and the Serial Shooter knew each other, as some were speculating. I did, however, feel they were feeding off the frenzy they had both created through the press, almost trying to "outdo" each other, if you will.

My reason for taking to the airwaves was simple: to get the public to be more aware of who lived next to them and to motivate the public to call in tips. I was spread so thin between the serial killers that I had to rely on the public's response, as did the police. As I had stated on KISS-FM while talking about the murderous spree the killers were on, the Phoenix Police Department was a first-rate team when it came to catching killers and they deserved our thanks, so thank you! My only intention in going public was to help draw out witnesses, apply pressure to the perpetrators, and give a time line for capture so people could rest easy again.

I then gave an interview to our NBC affiliate Channel 12 News to establish an arrest time line.

I was asked in July when the suspects would be arrested, and I said, "He will either be arrested in August or the police will know who they're dealing with in August." In August, as I had predicted, there were arrests made in the Serial Shooter case. Dale Hausner and Sam Dieteman were charged with the murders of many people and pets. It turned out that there had been two shooters working together, and they were arrested on August 3 to be exact. The Baseline Killer suspect Mark Goudeau was arrested on September 6, so it's understandable that I couldn't separate the suspects completely. In July, when I stated that "they would be arrested in August or the police would know who they're dealing with in August," it was really both of those. The police arrested the suspected Serial Shooters in August and the police also knew who they were dealing with concerning the Baseline Killer. It's not easy working cases in which your killers overlap both where and when they're killing. I've never worked another case where the killers would drive by and pick off people and animals for sport. Dieteman reportedly described it as "random recreational violence."

It's such a reinforcement of your own heart and soul's health when you read a story like this and are amazed at how anyone could be so cruel to innocent people. The Shooters were thrill killers just like the Baseline Killer was and had no conscience. The shooters were both driven by the same insatiable thirst for power and domination as I had said in my earlier television and radio interviews where I attempted to pinpoint the motives for both killers. It's hard to have any sympathy for these men, and I refuse to see such monsters overshadow their victims with their pleas.

The Baseline Killer and the Serial Shooters were not acquaintances, as some people were speculating. I felt that the killers didn't overlap and we were dealing with two different sets of killers. My time lines were correct, as were my profiles of them, and I could rest easy that the city I love was once again able to breathe. I was particularly affected by these two cases because they were happening on the streets that I grew up on and because the victims were so random and innocent. This wasn't a husband-and-wife dispute or a bar brawl gone bad; it was for sheer enjoyment and adrenaline rush on the killers' parts. That makes the killings more difficult to understand.

What kind of child grows up to be a predator? Is it in his genes? Is it a lack of parenting by his mom and dad? I think that it can be any or all of the above. Where science can't detect it, where parents won't see it, or somehow nature must make it, it's up to society as a whole to contain it. I am confident that the people who perpetuated these crimes will eventually get theirs.

There are many frustrations around my working a case, including garden variety obstacles and challenges that I face each time. With the Baseline Killer and Serial Shooters, my obstacle was crossing the information of the two cases. There were times that this happened, but ultimately the cases were resolved.

I worked a case recently that I was emotionally invested in; it may turn out to be my last. I spent a lot of time and energy going to crime scenes and meeting victims of the perpetrator, and in this case it wasn't the criminal who was the obstacle but rather office politics that hindered me. The detectives on the case were superb investigators, but unfortunately law enforcement is a politically charged field. When one egotistical cop caught wind of the help I had given the detectives, there was a political storm that threatened my friends in blue. I provided the name of the street that the perpetrator lived on and linked a crime that had never been tied to the string of other assaults. Even after that I was still being persecuted, but this time so were my friends. Anyone who knows me understands that loyalty is key to who I am, and I was not about to subject others to my plight. I walk the line between the living and the dead, I walk the line between the criminals and law enforcement. It's a balancing act. Even though my work had clear results, I had to walk away, and that was one of the hardest cases I ever worked because the faces of the victims were children whom I wasn't going to be permitted to help.

What do I do when something like this happens? I pray and I soul-search. As I've always said, "If I'm meant to help, it will be made possible." I believe that I'm only a messenger and no more than that. Even though it was hard for me to walk away from the case with all of those sexual assaults against little girls, it was the way it had to be because I couldn't have good cops penalized for working with me.

On a better note, when I get down because of the many obstacles that someone like me can face, I try and remember the happy endings. Yes, sometimes there are happy endings. I thought about a missing child case that I had worked on at the request of my husband. The granddaughter of one of Joe's coworkers was missing. I was rifling through jury questionnaires when Joe walked through the door. "Allison, I know how you are with your boundaries, but could you help me out?"

I thought maybe he had lost his car keys, so I was all set for the eye rolling of the century since I was not about to attempt to find them for him. Joe explained that his coworker's granddaughter had been missing for a few days and asked me to see if there was anything that I could get on her. It's usually very difficult to find somebody in a hurry, but in this case I could hear the words playing in my head telling me where she was. I said, "She's at her girlfriend's brother's apartment."

Joe asked me if I was sure, and then he called his coworker and passed on the information. The location that I sensed she was at was then passed on to the private investigator the family had hired. He re-interviewed the female friends of the missing girl and discovered that one of the girls remembered once being at the apartment of a friend's creepy brother. She had gotten a bad feeling while at the apartment, and she had called her dad and asked him to pick her up. The private investigator asked if she could re-member where this apartment was, and she said she'd try. So the private investigator tracked down the apartment that the young friend of the missing girl had visited, and when the door opened the miss-ing fourteen-year-old was there.

Joe still keeps in touch with the girl's family, and she's doing great. They had suspected the fourteen-year-old had been a runaway so the police weren't making her a priority. But as we all know, really bad things can happen to runaways, and she was a four-teen-year-old child.

I was attempting to weigh the pros and cons of what I do. I found a missing child, but my friends were being persecuted for doing their job and for being open to all resources that could help them solve a case. As of now I'm not sure that I will continue to work cases, but as the wise have often said, "Never say never!"

I will weigh what I've learned from the deceased in determining where I want to go with my life. First of all, I learned that's it's key not to squander your life, because many who've lived feel they missed the point of living by assuming that they'd always have more time. Often this is not the case, so you must make every day count. Also, what you do in life must fulfill you. Many people I've brought through in readings feel they should have taken more risks in life and they died unfulfilled because at some point in their life they started to live the way other people wanted them to. Instead of living from the inside going outward, they lived from the outside going in.

Second, how does it affect those around you who love you? Many of the messages from the deceased center around regretting not doing right by their family, so how we affect our family must be considered. When I work a case, it's unimportant to my kids and my husband whether it is successfully completed or left as unfinished business. They want to spend time with me and I must keep this in perspective, as we all should. So much can be learned from those who lived and died before us, and I know I give great importance to the wisdom of living. I've learned to live in the moment, love with all you have, and don't let others design who you are. You be the artist of you.

CHAPTER 3

Relationships and Being Your Own Best Friend

I've noticed in my readings that many of my clients lack faith in themselves, so I thought it necessary to write about learning to rely on oneself from time to time. Relationships come in a palette of different colors that can be mixed to make a breathtaking shade or an ugly mess. Through my readings I have observed a common theme in people's lives, and I see people make some similar and very basic errors. Through my experiences and common sense I'd like to comment on some of the most frequent "oopsies" that I've seen. In addition to commenting on these pivotal life "hinges," I want to reflect on my own relationships.

There are so many relationships that one can have, first our mom and dad, siblings, friends, other family members, acquaintances, coworkers, well, you get the picture. There are many people connected to each one of us, and we all affect each other. In childhood, I think a combination of elements helps to shape who we are in life and serves to define who we want to be.

For instance, I've seen people in childhood lose a loved one to cancer and then and there decide to become a doctor to help cancer patients. I think that when a young person watches someone she loves suffer and feels helpless because she can't save him, she has a tendency to choose a profession where she has more control over how she feels, or she might desire to sit in a position to affect how others feel. A lot of kids whose dads were police officers who passed away often join law enforcement themselves and pick up where their deceased parents left off. I find this a moving tribute as well as a way for the child to feel closer to the parent and carry on the legacy. So as children, our reactions to those from whom we do or do not feel love begin to shape our destiny.

I grew up knowing there was something different about me, even though I was like my friends in many ways. We all thought we had too much homework, we liked ice cream, the movies, and Fruit Stripe gum. I loved the things that made me more like my friends, yet I stood by my unique traits that made my friends look at me with questioning eyes.

Childhood is interesting because we grow to miss it and spend our lives trying to get over it. How ironic. My friends and I didn't understand grown-ups and we didn't really want to because we thought they took life way too seriously. It's funny how perspectives change. Even as young as eight years old I watched *60 Minutes* while my friends played TV tag in my front yard. I was told repeatedly this was not normal, but I knew that I wasn't the only kid who did things differently from her peers. When I met Joe, he told me that as a child he had watched it too, so there's my proof we were surely both born with old souls. It was no wonder that we found each other. Joe built his first computer at the age of eleven, so I don't doubt that he sacrificed playtime in order to learn something complicated.

Aside from being caught up in complex thoughts in my childhood, I was aware that other instances in my life were showing me what I was made of. I was sure that seeing my great-grandpa Johnson after his funeral when I was six years old had somehow changed my life because my mom didn't know how to respond to my vision. This reinforced my belief that I was walking a less traveled path and made me feel "strange" and not like other kids. I lost my beloved great-grandpa, and I knew that was when my life began to really take shape because death had now become a part of who I was.

Think back to who impacted your childhood and who took part knowingly or unknowingly in cultivating your destiny. It's important to realize that no matter where we came from, we all had moments in our young lives where we turned a corner and could never go back to the way it was before.

For me this was moving away from home just before my sixteenth birthday. Having grown-up responsibilities so early did help to shape who I am; it also made me a hard worker. That's okay; whether it was your own screwup or someone else's, you need to be your own best support and move forward out of love for yourself and those in your family who come after you. They want to know what you're made of so they can learn from your accomplishments as well as your mistakes; maybe it will spare them from encountering the same pitfalls, and that's a good thing.

I like to say, "Be your own best friend," because some people get a silly idea in their head that someone else needs to save them or "fix" them somehow, when all along only they can change themselves to be the best person they can possibly be. We are not someone else's project to "fix." For those with mental health issues, this doesn't apply. It's meant for people who are simply in a slump in life. Some people need mental health professionals, and that's an important part of their treatment in order to move forward in life.

For those of you out there who are just in a bad place, remember that if you have a void in your life, fill it with something that lifts you up to a higher level inside. I say this to those who look for love in all the wrong places. Who knows what you want or need better than you? Our partners can do only so much to make us feel special; the rest is up to us.

For instance, I know that I have a great husband and he tries so hard to make me happy. I realize that he can't read my mind and he's only human. I don't think that I'm so different from other women. I think most women like it when their partner knows what they're thinking and what they need emotionally. Once I truly understood this, I decided to court myself. I know that sounds odd, but follow me on this. I love to buy myself that special anything that makes me happy or treat myself to a manicure/pedicure and go to lunch with a friend. I've found that the more I do this for myself, the more fulfilled I become. The more fulfilled I am, the less pressure my family has as far as how to make me happy. My happiness shouldn't be a full-time job for them and vice versa. My friend Mary went out and bought herself a gorgeous diamond ring to celebrate her single status. How great is that?

I find that most women won't take their phone off the hook and give themselves a day of rest. A day of rest is a great soul booster to renew your spirit and incredibly necessary in order to give yourself the time to heal and reflect, and no one else will likely offer you this peace of mind. Spend your downtime any way you like to. I enjoy watching my DVD episodes of *Fantasy Island* with Mr. Roarke and Tattoo, who created a wonderful escape from the everyday gray; the TV show brings me back to my childhood, and that feels good to me.

Think about what makes you feel young inside and don't worry about what other people think of how you spend your recreational downtime, as long as it's legal (that's what we call a disclaimer): I've shared my silly secret so you don't have to feel so embarrassed by your own. This nurturing of one's soul is not limited to the ladies; men can give back to themselves too. They deserve the best care in the world, just like we do. Instead of waiting around for someone else to scratch an itch for you, you have yourself to do that. Who knows what her needs are more than the person who needs it?

Men deserve to be content, as we all do. A few suggestions for the men: Spoil yourselves with a full day of golf and don't apologize for not being somewhere else instead; book a massage and have a great lunch on "doctor's orders." If you're not into golf or spa treatments, then use your imagination and give yourself a greatly deserved break in life just for you. A man who's self-confident and relaxed is never alone for long. Trust me on this: the more that you invest in yourself—time, education, travel, culture, etc.—the more people you will draw to you.

I have a lot of men who have passed away who say that they never took the time to truly enjoy their lives, that they worked too much and played too little. So from all of the men I've experienced through readings who died, to all of the living men, don't forget to live while you can, live life fast-forward. These actions define who you are in life and death. When you invest in yourself, you're telling others that you're worth it. You're also nurturing your soul, making it more brilliant. This way when other quality people enter your life wanting to get to know you, you're not scrambling to make a mental list of jobs that person needs to do to "fulfill" you. If you're satisfied with who you are to begin with, then you don't settle for insufficient friendships or doomed relationships just to fill space around you.

Keeping these things in mind helps you to navigate your way through life more easily. Self-confidence, good character, and a sense of humor will make you a valuable person to know. The quality of self-confidence is not to be confused with arrogance. Arrogance says that all others are beneath you, whereas confidence says that you believe in yourself but want to know about others too, that you find great value in learning from others. Many people confuse those two characteristics.

Think about what I've said and see how it can best be applied to your life so that you don't burn out. It's a good way to feed your soul. Out of the thousands of readings that I've taken part in, I've never had a spirit come through and say that he should have worked more or spent less time lending a hand to someone in need. Being a good friend to others says a lot about your character; what kind of friends you have says a lot too.

Many people ask me how they can be a good friend to someone who has suffered a loss. Many don't know what to say under those strenuous circumstances, so I have some suggestions.

Making dinner for a friend who's suffered a great loss is never to be underestimated; it means the world to those who are in pain. Remember not to drop out of his life after the first week; mark your calendar on the same day every week. For instance, every Friday give him a call and see how he is. I noticed about a week after my dad died that the phone didn't ring so much and family members became silent. Honestly, I haven't heard from many of my dad's Arizona relatives since he died, so I'm using them as an example of what not to do. I ask you to try to do better than that.

I share personal details like this from my life for two reasons: first, so that others in the same boat don't feel so alone and understand that unfortunately it's common for families to divide after a death. My second reason is so others will try harder to sparkle as exceptional people and live better lives than some of the people I have observed in life. I hope they will show us that they are not all talk and no action as too many people are. I'm trying to inspire readers to be more action oriented in life and to allow themselves to be bothered but to tell their friend it's "no bother," to care sincerely about those around them even when it's inconvenient, because when someone you care about is asking for help, it should honestly be no bother to you. You will find yourself quickly addicted to wanting to connect with others and learn from their life stories as well as making some lifelong friends in the process.

Another way to elevate yourself to being the best that you can be is through charities. Even if it's only once a year, it still makes an enormous change in people's lives. So don't get bogged down thinking of your busy schedule and feeling guilty for having no time for others, because that doesn't do you any good and it's unnecessary. Mark off one day if that's all you have. It still shows great effort and huge character. Some people show they care by visiting an elderly person who lives alone and providing him or her with much desired company. Figure out what you enjoy and see how you can incorporate that into something that's mutually beneficial. There is no limit to the wonderful gifts that you have to offer the world. Remember your efforts create a butterfly effect.

I know what it is to be busy. I have a complicated schedule trying to balance family and work, so I have to be creative with how I can lend my energy to help others. For example, I appeared on a game show called *1 vs 100* on NBC to play for charity. I love game shows and I like helping people, so it was mutually beneficial. I was the last celebrity standing, which made me happy. I also had the chance to play alongside world renowned sex therapist Dr. Ruth and Academy Award–winning musicians Three 6 Mafia (I thought they were the most charming, down-to-earth guys). I also shared the panel with *Playboy* Playmates, which was a lot of fun for me because I know that my dad was definitely around; he would not have missed the opportunity to be near those lovelies. It was a great panel of people, and I think it's safe to say that they all had a fantastic time too.

I've learned that helping isn't always as much fun as a game show and it's not always easy, but it always, always feels good at the end of the day. I've also worked many painful cases over the last seven years for no money and at my own personal sacrifice just because I thought that it was the right thing to do. I've also helped friends when it's not as great a sacrifice but literally a headache! I've babysat for my friend's children while they're teething—enough said on that. Anyone knows that's a labor of love, but couples need time alone and so it is a seriously worthy favor that can renew a married couple's spirit. Now, that example was not a favor of monster proportions, yet it meant something to my friends. I sign books to be auctioned for charities; dinner with Joe and me at our favorite restaurant, the Rokerij, has been auctioned off more times than I can count; a "girls' night out" with me and eight of the auction winner's friends helped us to raise money for our daughter Aurora's school. Be creative. Your efforts can be fun and helpful at the same time.

I've had people do wonderful things for me too. Two weeks after my dad died, my friend Charles Shaughnessy (from the hit TV series *The Nanny*, and let's not forget that he played the hunky agent Shane Donovan on *Days of Our Lives*), who's one of the most genuine men that I've ever known, asked me if I wanted to come to the set and hang out with him since he had a return appearance on *Days.* He thought it would be a good distraction for me. A distraction was just what I needed and I loved *Days of Our Lives,* but the fact that he would take time out of his busy schedule to try to help an emotionally wounded friend meant the world to me. The trip was only a temporary distraction, but it is the sort of kindness that can make the biggest difference in someone's life, especially when he or she is at such a low point. What a guy!

Sometimes it seems to me that people who are emotionally wounded become invisible to everyone else because those whose lives are unshaken go into self-protection mode and don't want to get pulled into the other person's pain. The more you practice not seeing the people who suffer, the more disconnected you will become, until you care about very little. At the end of a life lived blindly, very few will care that the person is gone. So as a suggestion to all, although it can hurt spiritually and physically to empathize with those in pain, when you do this for others you make them stronger and in turn make yourself stronger for having cared.

What you do for others will come back to you tenfold, and being kind to others reflects on your "character," a much-forgotten word these days. I'd like to see the term make a comeback into our vocabularies. Remember, little gestures mean a lot and are sometimes the sweetest favors, so don't overlook them.

We've all heard someone say, "If I can help, just let me know, really." Well, that sounds good, but then you get in a jam and call on the offer just to hear, "Oh, I'm really busy, it's just not a good time for me," and when this is said out of laziness, that shows a lack of character.

The empty offer just makes the situation harder for the person who's reaching out for help. So to all of the good-intentioned people out there who never follow through on their helping hand, remember what the road to hell is paved with. Yeah, good intentions. This doesn't mean that there aren't times when a sincere attempt to help falls through. Stuff happens like a car accident and your hands are honestly tied. Anyone can understand that. I'm just illustrating characteristics in people that define how they're seen by others. People who always make promises but never keep them aren't valued by others.

On the flip side are those who burn themselves out living for anybody but themselves, and they lose themselves in others. I'm asking you to find a balance. It's okay to say no to people when you're spread too thin and it's affecting you mentally and/or physically. Boundaries are important in life, and those who never learn to create boundaries for themselves can become doormats.

Equally destructive are those who refuse to respect other people's boundaries and see the lines as invisible. They cross these lines frequently as they disregard people and hurt them by sucking the very life out of them. Everyone has known an "energy sucker" at some point in his or her life. I mean a negative energy that literally depresses you and steals your energy.

Look around you and determine who gravitates to you the most. Are they strong and independent, yet compassionate? If they are, then you have done a good job defining yourself because you most likely share those good traits and you know how to soothe your friends when they need a shoulder to lean on. If you're surrounded by people whose pattern in life is to ask to borrow money constantly, who believe that everyone in the world is out to get them, and generally serve as an energy drain for you, then you need to redefine who you are or else go down with the ship. Align yourself with people who are truly trying to better themselves and want to give back to your friendship. We were all born with the same capabilities to love and, for most, to work. As Ronald Reagan said, "The best socialized program is a job."

It's kind of like the "teach a man to fish" theory. You're helping a person more by assisting him in learning a skill or taking him to a job interview than by enabling him with "loans" that will never get paid back. If a man is hungry, you can keep sharing your fish with him, or you can teach him how to catch his own. It's your choice.

So to all the people out there making loan after

loan to family and friends, try taking them job hunt-
ing for a change or help them create a new résumé. It
really will help them more to pay their own bills, and
it will build their character as well as boost their confidence when they stop making excuses. You know
when a loan is life or death as opposed to your friend
wanting to pay her boyfriend's bail. Use your good
judgment and get it in writing if you do loan money
or anything of value. Contracts are exercised only
when someone defaults on the loan, so any upstand-
ing person will happily do the right thing and sign a
promissory note. Don't you feel guilty for asking for
one to be drawn up; it protects both parties involved.

As for Reagan, I couldn't agree with him more; it's
time for people to look back to their great-grandparents
and grandparents for guidance. They had many adversities, such as world wars and 50 percent mortal-
ity rates for their infants to deal with, yet most never
complained and they held their families close and
worked hard.

I came from a generation of latchkey kids and
single-parent households, so it's up to me to decide
what I want to pass on to my own kids. Just because
it was that way for me doesn't mean it has to be that
way for them. I'm making sure they feel loved and
safe, that they know how, as my dad always said, to
"laugh in the face of adversity." We've all been passed

a torch by someone in our family, and where we take it is up to us. I know some torches are easier to carry than others, but think about whether you want to be a martyr and destroy yourself or teach someone else how to carry that torch with pride so when it's passed it's easier for the next person to carry.

If everyone lived his or her life with the intention to make it better for those who follow, our world would be a far different place. There are many people who do live this way, and you can see the fruits of their labor in the enrichment of many others who've learned from them as well as the adoration shown through the sharing of memories that surround the person who lived to inspire.

My granddad inspired me to work hard and appreciate family, and also to be a little stubborn as well as proud. My grandpa Joe would have rather died than take a handout. Proud? Yes, he was, and at his funeral hundreds turned out to let us know what a great man he was. He was admired for his character, and he passed a torch to the rest of us that we're proud to carry through our own lives. He was able to give our family a shining example to follow and a granddad to look up to.

So to all those people out there who carry that "I just can't do it" energy, shake it off and reinvent yourself. People get into a funk, yet there are so many ways to feel good about your life. You don't have to be rich. My grandpa worked hard but wasn't wealthy; he left no trust fund. Family mattered to him and he had an incredible life because he cared about the people around him. I've learned a lot from my granddad, whose wisdom was simple and easy to understand. I paraphrase: "You give your word and you keep it. Remember that when you go out in the world you're a reflection of your family, so show the world what we're made of and make us proud."

What a guy! I share my granddad with you all because we learn from the wisdom around us, and he too can be learned from. Now, you won't see me buzzing around my neighborhood on a motor scooter going from one garage sale to the next—that was his bag, not mine. But I did learn to be my own person from him. He was cute, though, and he knew a bargain when he saw it! I see my grandpa Joe's apparition from time to time, but he gives me a wink and a nod and disappears because everything that he needed to say to me he did while he was alive. A couple of times right around the death of my grandma Lesa, Grandpa gave me messages to pass on to my uncle Joe and aunt Linda, but that's about it.

A characteristic I see in some people that can stunt the growth of your life is anger. The rage that some people carry through life can be frightening—the self-entitlement is deafening. We are all responsible for our own actions, so live life without regret. Don't be one of those people whom others fear or one who serves only to injure people in order to feel better about themselves. I've seen my share of adult bullies who might as well be name-calling on the playground as they puff up their chest to intimidate the smart kid. It's sad if you think about it, because they limit everyone around them.

My mom always liked the story of me in kindergarten at Larkspur Elementary School when a third-grade boy pushed me backward off a big cement tunnel. I started to cry, then I brushed off my dress and walked up to him and socked him in the stomach. He was taken to the nurse's office, and I was satisfied, even with the big lump on the back of my head. He was treated for his stomachache and then expelled from school. I never heard him again taunt me about my red hair.

Now, I'm not saying you should sock your bully, but I grew up to be a woman who can recognize bullies when I see them, and no matter how old they are they all look the same. Standing up for yourself in life when it really matters is an important part of drawing the line so that others know that you have limits. It's all a part of taking care of yourself. Because how can you love others or understand why they love you if you can't love yourself?

Every day we interact with others, and there are

windows of opportunity to make someone's life easier or harder. Whether or not you take the opportunity says something about where you are in your life. I personally find that easing another person's mind not only feels right, it also feeds my soul. My advice is, try extending yourself in a moment when things in your life aren't great for you and see how quickly your life starts to improve. Some people do so much for others that they feel like they can never do enough. I'm lucky enough to know some of these exceptional humanitarians. Many of us will be lucky if we meet only one person like this in our lifetime, someone who looks at the world through different eyes from the rest.

For those of you who aren't sure how you've helped another person, reach out today to someone who needs a little kindness. Reach and teach: if everyone reaches out to help another and then teaches this to his children or someone he knows, imagine the phenomenal butterfly effect that would have on the world. I always appreciate when a stranger smiles at me for no reason other than to connect with me. There's nothing she wants except a friendly smile in return, which I willingly give. I am pleased to know by my readers' responses that they care about living a better life and that they appreciate the great moments they've had so far. Just by reading my book, you say that you are on the same search that I am, which is to understand death so that you can live a better life.

Try not to carry too much emotional baggage with you through your life—you just end up passing it to others. And, of course, the ultimate search is for living your life to its absolute, busting-at-the-seams fullest. People are multifaceted, capable of being many things. I'm a medium, a wife, a mother, a friend. I've been on task forces, I'm a fund-raiser for charities, I'm an author of three books—and I'm not done! I still want to increase my knowledge of foreign languages and I want to learn how to play the theme from *Somewhere in Time* on the piano. Why? Because it would make me happy, that's why, and it's enough of a reason to do it. This is not all that I've done or all that I am; it is only a part of my life, and I will continue to do and be more.

There is an art to cramming many lives into the one that you have: be what you feel drawn to, do the right thing, have what you feel would mean something to you and, most important, help others to do the same. It's our legacy, it's why we are here and, much like the monarch butterfly, we will make only part of our migration in this life. But we pass the torch to those who come after us to continue to push forward, and we have in reality passed on to them the fire that burned in our eyes and our hearts, it's in fact our soul.

Many times I've brought a parent through for a child, and the mom or dad will show me the kid looking in the mirror and the reflection of the parent looking back with a wink and a smile. Often the parent will say, "If you need to see me, just look in the mirror and I'm there." Our loved ones are never truly gone from us. They remain in the landscape of our own life, as we will for those who come after us. So do right by them by celebrating your own greatness as well as remembering theirs.

CHAPTER 4

Family Matters

*W*ell, I think that this title is self-explanatory; my chapter title goes along the same line as my book title *Secrets of the Monarch*. The significance lies in family/friends and how we affect each other's life. This can be from parent to child or many other family connections. In my case, I was passed a torch or a "job" to do from Domini for her unfinished business among the living.

Many of you have read in my books *Don't Kiss Them Good-bye* and *We Are Their Heaven* about my childhood friend Domini. I met Domini when I was fourteen years old at our school bus stop in front of North High. That moment led to a friendship that later made us roommates and even bonded us through my writing this book. When we were teenagers (Domini was two years older than me), we went to see the movie *Beaches* together and she asked me then to promise that if something happened to her, I would be a part of her little girl's life and tell her stories of who her mom was.

I gave Domini a hard time about the bizarre thought that she wouldn't be here, but then I relented and I agreed to the pact. I was young and it was hard to imagine one of my friends ever dying before her hair had turned gray. I was eighteen when Marissa was born, and I remember holding her for the first time, my friend's little girl. She had bright red hair and baby blue eyes that looked like her mother's.

Around that time I took Domini to the doctor and she had a cyst removed from her ovary. I told Domini that she needed to take better care of herself or she'd pass away around the age of thirty. Domini didn't even flinch; she trusted what I said but continued to live life her way—that was Domini. Marissa was my first real attempt at changing a toddler's diaper, and I put it on her backward. I was a youngest child, so I thought that Happy Meals were somehow the universal antidote to make the young stop crying. (Obviously I've got different parenting skills now!) I met Joe two years later, and Domini's life and mine took different directions.

Years later I had a strong urge to locate Domini, and I set out on the internet to find her. I ended up finding Marissa's dad, Dominic, Domini's ex-husband. After all my detective work I finally got in touch with Domini, and she told me that she was pregnant and remarried. Sadly, a year after I found Domini, she died from melanoma at the age of thirty-one. While she was dying she reminded me of my promise to her all those years ago as we watched *Beaches*, the promise that I'd made her concerning Marissa. When Domini died, Marissa was only eleven years old.

Now fast-forward five years. Joe and I were sitting on our patio talking about Marissa's up-and-coming sixteenth birthday party. I looked up because something had caught my eye. Domini was leaning against one of our patio pillars, smiling at me. I was so happy to see her because she showed herself to me only once or twice a year. I figured that she had come because it was around her birthday, Dominic's birthday, and also Marissa's; they were all born in November.

Even in death, Domini had the same sparkling eyes, her hair was down, and she wore a black skirt and top with shoulder pads, which I recognized as one of hers from around 1988. Bright white smile—check; devilish air about her—intact; the look in her eyes as though she knew something that I didn't—yep, it was all there per usual. I explained to Joe what was going on and he laughed. He knew Domini too, and we both missed her. I noticed that she was wearing a pair of my old black pumps.

I said, "Domini, why are you wearing my shoes?"

Her smile turned serious and she said, "I just wanted to see what it's like to walk a day in your shoes, Ali."

She then disappeared as quickly and abruptly as she had come. And what the hell did she mean by that, anyway, a day in my shoes?

Well, I was grateful for the visit from Domini, and I was quite sure that whatever Domini meant by her words would reveal itself to me later. Marissa's sweet sixteen was approaching and I wanted to do something special for her. Immediately I saw a picture in my head that would include Marissa and her parents. I called Dominic and asked him for a picture of himself and Domini and Marissa when Marissa was a baby. He found the perfect one. I decided to have the picture scanned onto Marissa's birthday cake so that Marissa could see her mom at her party, and Domini would be front and center. Marissa decided that she wanted her party at a roller-skating rink, and that I could do. I love skating! Her party was going to be at the Great Skate Roller Rink that I used to compete at when I was a kid. I thought, "How cool is that!" I was feeling a little overzealous and I rented out the whole rink just for Marissa. I had kept my promise to Domini to be there for Marissa, and her sixteenth birthday party was going to be the day that I could really feel I'd kept a big part of my teenage vow. Was it even possible that Marissa was sixteen and my friend Domini was dead? It all seemed so impossible, but I'm not the only person in the world to feel this way, I know that.

Marissa's party was a very happy occasion, but there was a feeling that something or someone was missing. I unveiled the cake to Marissa and, as you can imagine, she drew her hand gently to her mouth, and in that moment of celebration Marissa looked as though she was seeing her mother for the first time in five years. With tears in her eyes, she said, "I know my mom's here."

I nodded my head. "Yes."

I watched my daughter Aurora and Marissa speed-skate into the photo booth at the skating rink and giggle as they took pictures together. It was just as Domini and I had planned when we were teenagers, as many young girls do. We were going to raise our girls together and they would be friends like we were. I flashed back again to the characters in *Beaches*. The two friends who were going to set the world on fire as kids on the pier taking a picture together in a photo booth just like the one our girls were sitting in now. These are the pictures that they would keep forever. I thought, "How ironic is that?"

Our girls came bolting out of the booth, racing back to the skating-rink floor. All I could think was, "Man, I miss Dom."

People think that because I'm a medium it doesn't hurt to miss people who have died. But that's not true. I have a deeper understanding that they are still here, but in a different form, but that doesn't mean that I don't miss the way things were before they died.

I was leaning against the wall away from the group because my having had the honor of slicing the cake and then serving it to the kids was emotionally difficult for me. Marissa called out, "I want the piece of cake with my mom and me on it!"

I said, "You got it, baby!"

Seeing my friend on the cake as a tribute to her daughter was haunting and heart wrenching. I was also very proud to be the one who could make this day happen for Marissa and Dom. I composed myself, and I sort of cursed nature for giving me tears and a heart that could ache. Joe walked up behind me and put his hand on my shoulder. He seemed kind of excited and said, "Allison, I know what Dom meant about standing in your shoes. Domini meant that she is not *heard* or understood by all because she stands in the shoes of the dead, and so do you. Today you stood in Domini's shoes when you acted in her place for her daughter. You planned the party, served the cake, bought Marissa the special birthday outfit to wear, and reminded her that she is loved. So today you stood in each other's shoes."

A wonderful smile spread across my face as it resonated within me that Joe was right. When Domini was alive, she couldn't fully understand what it was like to see the otherside and live with it, because it was a part of me that she couldn't experience. After her death, she was able not only to see the otherside, but she became a part of it as well, just after her death instead of in her life like me.

Wow! His analogy made sense and I knew that he was right. Pretty good, Joe!

I was too close to Domini to get her riddle, but Joe wasn't. Boy, I am a lucky girl to have a husband who can see outside the proverbial box!

Just when I thought I had weathered my emotional storm, the DJ played "I Will Survive" by Gloria Gaynor, which as my readers know is Domini's calling card. This was particularly funny because Marissa had requested that the DJ strictly play alternative yet top forty–type music like Green Day and Avril Lavigne, a sort of skateboard punk music, if there's such a thing. That's what it sounded like to my adult ears, anyway. Well, disco was a far cry from that, so I asked Dominic if he had requested that song. He shook his head, and part of me wanted to revert back to my teen years and call Domini a not-so-nice name—in jest, of course, with a shifty grin on my face. Instead I smiled. I knew that Domini was just making sure that we knew that she was a part of Marissa's special day. Listening to that song at the party it seemed to go on forever in slow motion, but it finally drew to an end.

I was in a daze and the party was winding down. Many hot dogs, sodas, pizzas, and teenage songs later, Marissa's birthday had achieved the status of an unforgettable party. She was beaming with joy and importance, and I loved it. There's no doubt in my mind that my bright party ideas were not completely my own. Domini always loved a good time, and that day was a long time coming. Domini had passed me the torch that involved being there for her daughter when she physically couldn't, and I gladly ran with that torch. That day it also became clear to me that Domini had passed her love of life and her belief in life after death on to her daughter Marissa.

DOMINI STRIKES AGAIN!

I often talk to people about the unbelievable amount of power that the deceased have on the otherside and that things are not always as they seem.

Domini died on April 2, 2001, and it had been almost six years since she had passed away; one week shy of six years, to be exact. Although Domini and Dominic had divorced and she had remarried, Dominic took care of Domini for the last few months of her life. Her new husband quickly left the picture when she became ill, and Dominic reentered Domini's life.

There was a local radio contest in Phoenix that I had heard of two days before it ended. The prize was a new car, and the object of the contest was to see who could get the most celebrities to call in to the radio station. Had I known that this contest had been running for almost two weeks, I wouldn't have agreed to help Dominic try to win the car for our Marissa, who had just turned sixteen a few months prior. I called in as many markers as I could to get celebrities to call in to the station, but there were other contestants who had impressive celebs call in too, so it was a steep competition and they had a two-week head start.

I had such an all-consuming passion, drive, if you will, to win this contest because I felt like Domini was pushing me to help Dominic with everything I had. It was almost as if she were fueling me to do this. I knew that Domini had never had a new car, and I could feel that she wanted Marissa to have what she hadn't because that's what parents who love their kids all want for them, whether it is material comfort or emotional affection. I knew that Domini was "pulling the strings," and I talked to her and told her that she'd better do everything in her power to help me from the otherside because I am only one person and I was getting a late start in the contest. I didn't know how late until the day they read the winner's name on air.

I was able to get the Arquette clan to call in, which didn't surprise me because Patricia has such a big heart. Even though she was busy on a media tour she still cared enough for Marissa to take the time to call in for her. Patricia had lost her own mom to cancer, so she empathized with Marissa on a deep level. I was able to get a few others to call in, and I crossed my fingers and prayed with all I had. The next day the winner was read on the air, and it was not us. On one hand I was relieved that it was over, but on the other hand I felt like I'd failed Domini and Marissa both, and the anniversary of Domini's death was just three days away.

Joe and I went out to lunch to clear our heads and fill our stomachs. While we were at lunch, Joe's cell phone rang. Apparently, while on her media tour, Patricia Arquette had mentioned the contest to a fellow actor who was touched by Marissa's story. This woman had also lost her mom to cancer at a young age. By the time this fellow actor had called in to the radio station, the contest had ended and she was disappointed. Joe turned to me with a blank look on his face. So I asked him, "Who was it?"

"Allison, I have a phone number for you to call. It's the personal assistant's number. She works for a celebrity and she wants to talk to you."

For my readers who are wondering why I don't name the celebrity, understand that she doesn't want credit for her good deed, she's humble. I'm also quite sure that she doesn't want to buy the whole world a car, and I can understand that too. I called the assistant, who was a smart, upbeat young woman. She told me whom she represented, and then she blew my mind.

"Mrs. DuBois, my boss wants me to buy Marissa a car."

"What? Are you kidding me?"

"No, I'm serious. What kind of car was given away in the contest?"

"It was a 2007 Mitsubishi Spyder convertible," I said with I'm sure the most shocked look on my face as I absorbed the magnitude of the gesture of kindness. I was stunned that this was even happening but grateful. I also gave kudos to Domini. So many events had to take place in order to make this moment possible that I know Domini literally had moved mountains. The car would be delivered on April 2, the six-year anniversary of Domini's death. The timing was uncanny.

Let's look at the series of events that had to occur in order for Marissa to get this car. The radio station had to have the contest and the prize had to be a car, or it would have been pointless for Dominic to enter and pointless for me to help. I had to hear about the contest by listening to the station that was having it. The timing of Domini's death had to be important to me so that I felt compelled to do this for her and help Dominic round up celebrities to accomplish this. I had to know Patricia Arquette. She had to care about me enough to do this for me. She had to be on the morning show that day of all days to try and get a particular fellow celeb to call in for Dominic/Marissa while there was still time. Patricia and her fellow actor both lost their moms to cancer and they empathized with Marissa who lost her mom when she was only eleven years old. So many things had to happen to bring that car to Marissa and let her know that she mattered to these two very accomplished women who were also mothers, whom Domini succeeded in touching.

I always say that if the deceased need something to be done for a living loved one, they will work through living people to get the desired result. Those of us who listen to the deceased with our hearts and minds take part in letting their existing souls affect our lives in a positive way and guide us down the right path for us and those we love. In a strange way, a reversal of roles, if you will, allows the deceased see those who listen to them as sort of "angels on earth," because we help to carry out their emotional wishes in helping others, so it's really special to have a chance to take part in an event that changes a life for the better. Domini worked through me to love her daughter and inspire others to pay attention, because the dead are able and willing to continue loving us through their efforts and energy.

I was informed that the car would be delivered to Marissa's house with a big red bow on it and a note from Patricia and her fellow celebrity attached to the windshield. That day would be memorable not only because my friend Domini had died that day or because her daughter was receiving a huge token of affection from two powerful and loving women.

On the way to the surprise for Marissa, I received a phone call. It was from my good friend Johnjay, who is a morning show host for KISS-FM, the station that held the contest to win the car. He informed me that his dad, whom I affectionately called "Big John," had just died. I was floored and deeply distraught for Johnjay and his family. His dad reminded me a lot of my own, whom I missed so much; they were both vibrant ladies' men and they were the life of any party. There were some things that just didn't add up around Big John's death, so I told Johnjay to make sure to "treat it like a crime scene" just in case, because you can never really go back once the evidence has been tainted. Sometimes it's one variable that cracks a case wide open, and we want to make sure that the scene is well preserved. So the day that I didn't think could get any stranger had done just that. Now Big John shared his day of passing with my friend Domini and now the day held even more meaning to me. I stared out the window and tried to imagine how my friend Johnjay was feeling, and then it occurred to me that I knew exactly how he was feeling.

Johnjay reminded me weeks later about us having lunch together in Pinetop, Arizona, the December prior to his dad's passing, which was about three months before his dad's death. "Allison, you grabbed my arm when we were leaving and told me to make sure that my dad got his heart checked out."

I recalled the moment he spoke of and mentally noted that the medical examiner had told Johnjay's family that Big John had died of heart disease, but at the same time I didn't want Johnjay to feel at all responsible for his dad's passing. Kids have a way of carrying guilt when they lose a parent. I saw Big John's passing a lot like my own dad's. It was "not preventable"; sometimes no amount of intervention will change what was to be.

There were some interesting similarities in our dads' deaths, almost like mirror images of each other. Our dads died almost exactly six months apart, my dad on September 22 and his on April 2. My dad's sign to me has always been 222, and if you look at the dates, it's 222. Those of you who have read my previous books know how important those numbers are to me. My dad died in Arizona on September 22, 2002, while I was at my cousin Vanessa's wedding in California. I had to fly home to make the arrangements for him. Johnjay was in Arizona and his dad was in California, so his flight was the reverse of mine. Johnjay had just moved into a new house in Phoenix and was still unpacking boxes. I had also moved to a new house in Phoenix and my dad died three weeks after I moved there. Neither of our dads ever crossed our threshold while he was alive. His dad passed from heart failure as did mine, and neither one of our dads had previously had heart problems. They were both found in the same room of the house the next morning by their girlfriends. His dad was Dutch and married Johnjay's mom, who's Mexican; my dad was Hispanic and married my mom, who was German. I told Johnjay that we should go to my Halloween party as the "ambiguously Mexican duo" because neither of us looks Latino, but we both looove the food! So we have very similar backgrounds. Our dads were both very cool, and our friends often commented that they wished they'd had a dad like ours. I'm one of two kids, a boy and a girl; so is Johnjay, who has a sister. Johnjay and his wife, Blake, have three sons and Joe and I have three daughters.

els. It's comforting, in a way, to know that I have a friend where our families just click. There's no real explanation; we were brought together for a reason. I met Johnjay when he interviewed me two and a half years ago for his morning show, and the rest is history. If you've been lucky enough to cross paths with someone who makes you feel "at home," like you'd known each other your whole life, then you've been blessed. This goes for his or her ability to irritate you as well as sharing a comfort zone.

So back to Marissa. I finally arrived at Marissa's house with Joe and our eldest daughter Aurora, who had grown up with Marissa. She wanted to see Marissa's face light up too. We positioned our Ford Expedition so that it would hide the new car, which was headed down the street toward us. It was a breathtakingly beautiful candy apple red 2007 Mitsubishi Spyder convertible that had the grown-ups feeling a bit envious. We parked it in the driveway and placed a poster board with a collage of Domini's photos on it in the passenger seat. I tucked my card to Marissa adjacent to the one sent by the gift givers, and we waited for Marissa to get off her school bus. We knew she was in for the shock of her life. Our friend Randy Stein from KISS-FM was there to record the moment to play back for their listeners. Marissa's dad was as happy as I'd seen him in the six years since Domini's death. Two nice guys from Chapman

Chevrolet on Bell Road, who were responsible for covering tax, license, and registration were there with big grins on their faces and sweat on their brows, but they didn't mind because a girl was about to get the surprise of a lifetime.

Finally Marissa's bus pulled up and she saw the group of grown-ups in front of her house. She looked nervous, which I can understand. She had a friend with her and I started walking toward them and I waved. She said, "Oh, I didn't know it was you."

My response was, "Oh, yeah, I only used to change your diapers and I've known you your whole life. I can understand how that could happen." I was just giving her a hard time; she was pretty far away when she got off the bus and it'd be hard to identify anyone at that distance. Why do grown-ups like to embarrass kids by pulling the "diaper" card, anyway? Arrgghh. Now I'm one of them!

I began explaining to Marissa why we were there. "Marissa, you know how we tried really hard but we didn't win the car from the contest?" She nodded. "One of Patricia Arquette's celebrity friends," I said as I turned her toward the car, "bought you an identical car."

She began crying and obviously was in disbelief. I went on. "They both lost their moms to cancer at a young age and they wanted you to know that they know what you're going through and that you matter to them."

There wasn't a dry eye among us, and I knew that my friend whom I missed so much and I had worked together just like old times and achieved what seemed impossible. We videotaped and photographed Marissa receiving her new car so that we could send it to the two women who had been so unbelievably caring. Marissa looked at us and said, "This is the happiest day of my life."

Taking in that her mom died on that day, only something so selfless and from women who understood Marissa's painful loss could make April 2 become the "happiest" day of her life. Aurora jumped into the passenger seat next to Marissa, and as I took their picture, Dominic said, "Allison, it looks like you and Domini. When you met you were about the same age; she was sixteen and you were fourteen."

Tears welled up in my eyes as I noticed that, wow, they did both look exactly like their mothers; life had come full circle. I'm sharing this story for two reasons. One, because we see so much bad on the news that sometimes we lose sight that there are good people in this world who really do care about the people around them. For us it was the philanthropist who gave Marissa the car, the dealership that covered expenses, and the family that Marissa will always have that loves her. Two, to demonstrate the love and power that the otherside has and bestows upon us every day. Look what Domini went through to orchestrate this and the lengths that Patricia and her friend's moms and countless others who've passed went through to touch a child, be inspired, believe that they are not gone.

A footnote. Where one circle had been completed, I now had someone else that I had to be there for until he too can feel his dad again. The circle had been completed on April 2, and the torch had been passed that day from one child who had lost a parent (Marissa) to another child who had just lost his dad (Johnjay). Marissa left a message for Johnjay on Randy's handheld recorder saying that "she knew how he felt" and offering condolences and friendship. It moved us all, because it came from a sixteen-year-old girl who was not angry at the world for taking her mother but instead wanted to help others to understand that our loved ones never truly die. They continue to be with us whenever we need them, as her mom was with her that day.

CHAPTER 5

Passing Torches: The Family Evolution

*W*hen Domini passed her belief in the otherside and her love of life on to Marissa, she demonstrated the good "torches" that we all can choose to pass on to our kids rather than passing them the bad ones like drug addiction, memories of words that should never have been spoken, or parents who weren't there for them.

Consider what sort of an impact you want to make on the people in your life and how you want to be remembered. Part of the reason I wanted to write this chapter is that I don't think everyone understands we have the power to affect someone else's entire life. If you think about it, we've all heard stories of family members who died before we were born, and we can see the effects that they had on our parents, grandparents, etc., good and bad.

When I read clients and a relative who's passed away comes through with a message for the living, it affects them in different ways. I've seen clients turn into wounded children again right before my eyes. I've seen daughters whose deceased father has come through with an apology for not being there for them in life. I've seen women start yelling at their deceased father and then turn to me with unforgiving eyes as they explain that it's too late for an apology now. I've seen daughters tear up and softly smile as they hear words that they've waited their whole life to hear.

As a parent, you have a choice of how you will be received after your death by your child. Some parents are lucky that there were enough good memories in their child's life that the bad ones could be forgiven. Some parents aren't so fortunate, so as we raise our kids, let's remember to make them feel loved now so that after we die they will feel loved by us forever. It's now or never.

There are tools we can give to our kids that will extend through many generations. One of the tools that I was able to pass on to our girls was the ability to persevere by showing them that there are times when a painful experience can be adjusted so that it no longer can continue to hurt us. For instance, when my dad died, the only thing I really wanted of his was a large oil painting that he had painted of me when I was two years old. Some angry family members were mad that I inherited his bank account, and the picture mysteriously disappeared from my dad's house. When I asked about the painting, one of my relatives said, "Maybe it was accidentally thrown away!"

She said it with such a sneer and disdain for me that it was bordering on hate. I understand what people who suffer great loss go through. My dad's stuff had long been picked over before I ever got to his house because his family felt entitled, and many things were missing. Like I've always said, death can bring out the best or the worst in people. I'd always miss that painting, so I came up with a way to make a painful act right for me. My dad loved my three girls more than anything, so I decided to take a picture of each of my daughters and have a portrait gallery paint them each an oil painting that they could love like I had loved mine.

Sophia has a beautiful painting now of herself at four years old dressed up like Miss America, crown on her head and all. She was born on the fourth of

July, and I know she will love this painting throughout her life, as will her children. Right now Sophia lies in bed at night and stares at her painting until she falls asleep with a little angel grin on her face. Fallon has a painting of herself in her white first communion gown with an enchanting tiara that makes her feel like a princess. I know she will cherish it always. Aurora, my oldest, has a painting of herself in her sixth grade blue and gold cheerleading uniform, and I smile every time I see it.

I may not have the portrait of the two-year-old little me, but I have been able to rid myself of the resentment and the pain caused by certain family members by providing my girls with such a special gift from their grandpa that truly makes me happy.

I remember every detail of my painting since I had stared at it my whole life, and I felt special to my dad because he took the time to paint me when I was small. No one can ever take that love or memory away from me. In addition to that gratification, the portrait studio I had hired needed four or five months to complete the paintings. They came in on Christmas Eve, which is my dad's birthday. I know that it was his way of saying that he was happy with the paintings and that they were without a doubt from him. I didn't get the one for me, but he sent me three more for my girls to make it right.

Life becomes much easier when you learn to make

energy "adjustments" that will help to right a wrong for you. People everywhere are faced with hardships, and some people deal out the pain and some people receive the energy that was dealt. What I've learned is that we are all forces of nature and we have the wonderful ability to merge our intelligence with our emotions and determine what works for us, what makes sense in our head as well as what resonates with our soul. So here's my suggestion: any emotional event that wounded your soul needs to be dealt with. Some achieve their balance through therapy or yoga, and some of us must learn to be creative and fix it.

I don't mean that the bad memory will ever fully leave you, but there are ways to take the power away from the bad memory and energetically replace our pain with a positive result instead. I know many great people whose children have died prematurely. They've created organizations to help other parents move forward and to act as support for those who walk their same path. They know they can't bring their baby back, but they can hold the hand of someone who needs another parent who understands their pain when no one else can. Talking to the parents, I've learned that the pain we carry inside of us acts as a sort of "spiritual cancer" and can be released little by little through acknowledging that pain and honoring the person we miss so much.

In my first book, *Don't Kiss Them Good-bye,* I wrote a chapter around my dad's death, and it was honest to God physically painful for me to write. I've found that every time someone approaches me and tells me that my father's story helped her with the loss of her own parent and how she could relate to my raw state of emotion, I am able to let go of some of that pain and replace it with joy. Not joy that my dad's gone— I'd do just about anything to bring him back—but joy because I know how happy it makes my dad to help others and to learn, every time a son or daughter reads his story, of how much fathers mean to their kids. In turn this allows him to fully appreciate how much I loved him and who he was in my eyes.

When people die, they learn how much they meant to their family and friends. When they are also memorialized in some way, they connect with every person their story continues to touch. For them it's almost like having box seats in an arena and seeing a lot of people affected all at once. For those who aren't memorialized, this doesn't mean that they don't touch people. They find ways to connect with the living if it matters to them. Some people who pass away don't have the need to connect with strangers, and that's more than fine. My point is that we all have the ability to connect or not to connect, both in life and death.

So don't lend power to negativity. Instead, learn

how to replace pain with something that will soothe your soul. Like our bodies, our souls also need annual checkups, so don't neglect your spiritual well-being. Use the lessons that you're taught in life to live better and be good to yourself because you're passing life tools on to younger generations.

Growing up, I was always aware that some of my family members had issues, and I found a way in my life to do right by myself and my family and to pass a healthy, loving environment on to my girls. Don't get me wrong, many of my family members are great and wonderful people. It's only a small handful that I could do without. You know what I mean—everyone's family has at least one sour grape. Having a family of my own has taught me what "family" is all about; sometimes it's up to us to redefine happiness when our childhood was someone else's idea of happy and never felt quite right.

There is no end to the great memories I have of my husband and daughters, and I am in a unique position to share in other people's family memories almost as a voyeur. I've seen the living left with so much baggage by those who have died that I don't even know how they carry it all. On the flip side, I've seen the deceased leave the living with nothing less than pure love and positive energy. I know that I will continue to invest emotionally in my kids not just because I love them more than anything but because the love I give them now will translate into energy that they can draw from later in life. It's almost like giving them the power they will need in the future now so they can use it when they're low on energy. They will be able to take from the positive energy that I gave them in life and use it to fuel themselves forward when they need it the most.

I made the simple decision long ago to leave my kids with as much of the good stuff as I can possibly muster for them. I feel very deeply for kids whose parents invested no energy in them or constantly directed negative energy at them. This was no fault of the child's but was due to a parent who didn't cope well with life and relationships. This child can take all of the negativity dealt him by the parents and allow that to fuel him forward in a positive manner, or he can let it destroy himself from the inside out.

It takes great strength and belief in oneself to become a complete person when you've been presented with so many obstacles. It is possible to come from a bad place in life and turn it all around and make yourself into the person you've always wanted to be. I've met people who lived through traumatic, horrible childhoods and turned out to be the most unselfish, shining examples of how good humanity can be. I know that in my life the adversities I faced helped to form who I am today, and for that I'm thankful. My parents were divorced, so what? When I was growing up I had no memory of them ever being together, so honestly there was no pain there for me, but it did make me more independent and a critical thinker because I was privy to what "divorce" and "child support" were.

Many things aren't explained to kids by their parents, so the kids start to investigate and really think about the details they've pieced together through overhearing adults talk when they think their kids are asleep. So these moments in my life caused me to trust my instincts because I learned that sometimes grown-ups say one thing and do something different. Understand that everyone has been made either to grow up too fast or learn a lesson about life the hard way. It's the friction that allows us to evolve, and whether we make a positive out of it or a negative is up to us. If you go through life feeling sorry for yourself, you miss the point of living.

I think that most people sense there is something great inside of them. We are all blessed with some sort of gift or special position in life, and I think many people feel that no one else seemed to see it in them, but of course that doesn't mean it wasn't there all along. Don't look to your family, neighbors, and friends for approval, or even to the other parents at your child's school. Only you have to approve of yourself—no one else should stop you from reaching for who you want to be in life. Weigh your strengths and weaknesses. I feel that there is something that guides us from within, and those who listen to the guidance often live inspiring lives.

Two people with the same upbringing can be totally different in their beliefs and personalities. There are many variables that influence why they are so different. I believe one variable is their ability and desire to access their soul. People become very distracted by the hustle and bustle in the world and they begin to focus on what's outside of them rather than what they hear inside. It's so important to listen to your inner self, or your soul sort of gets backed up from not being nurtured. So as you go through your day, remember to take some time for yourself where you're in a quiet place of reflection.

I like to listen to jazz music and let the notes run through me. It's healing and it feels like the music repairs my soul in a way. I call it "getting in my zone"; others call it quiet contemplation or meditation. Whatever you call it, it's good for you. It's a wise idea to take inventory of how you feel inside to know that you're on the path on which you belong. "Soul searching," if you will, can help you to live a much happier life as long as you listen to your truth without editing it to fit what your mind would rather do.

I often close my eyes and visualize my internal health. I visualize myself, starting at the top of my head and ending at the bottom of my feet. If at any time while I'm visualizing my health I find myself focusing in on one particular area, I know that it's time to go to the doctor. Besides getting regular check-ups, it's also important to listen to your body and take the time to make sure that your body, mind, and soul are simpatico. This is an effective exercise for anyone who's interested in physical well-being.

On one occasion, and, mind you, I am sharing this only hoping to inspire others to listen to their internal dialogue, I had a doctor's appointment. This appointment was with the doctor most women dread going to see (you know what I mean). For men the equivalent is a prostate exam, not much fun! I canceled it because I just didn't want to go, even though I know it is important to have an annual checkup. I said to myself, "If there's something wrong with me, I'm sure I'll get a sign." I smirked and I knew that I was just being a big baby who was trying to play hooky from the doctor.

Well, it was weighing heavy on my mind, but I was still being stubborn. A few weeks later I went with some girlfriends to Las Vegas for some much-needed fun and relaxation. The girls and I were boarding the plane in Las Vegas to return home to Phoenix, and I glanced across the aisle and who do you think I saw? Yep, it was the doctor I had been trying to avoid for the last few weeks! Not only did I have to laugh, because there couldn't have been a more obvious sign, but it also made me nervous because I knew there was something wrong with me if my guides were going to such great lengths to get me in to see the doctor. I approached the wonderful Dr. Trachtenberg, who had delivered all three of my darling daughters, and said the dumbest thing. "Hey, Dr. Trachtenberg, how are you? It so good to see you and I look forward to seeing you again."

Why is this stupid? Because the only time I would see him again would be in his office, and I'm quite sure he feels no excitement about our next visit. Not only that, but his wife was sitting next to him and she didn't look happy about my enthusiasm. My nervousness had made me seem a little high-strung. I'm sure that women will empathize with me on this one.

Anyway, when I returned I made an appointment, and it turned out that I did have some abnormal, potentially precancerous cells that needed to be removed, and it would require an outpatient procedure. Needless to say, the procedure was successful, and as I came to I was feeling groggy from the anesthetic. I remember the look on the nurse's face when I started telling her about all of the dead people around her. She laughed and told me that the medication sometimes makes people see things, and I matched her laugh with my own because I knew that what I saw had nothing to do with the medication.

I was given a bill of good health, and now I try to be less of a baby about going to the doctor. See, I learned my lesson. I'm being candid with you because these life lessons are vital to our well-being and my somewhat embarrassing story is nothing when compared to how many people it might help in the long run. I teach these lessons of listening to one's inner self to my girls, helping them to be more tuned in to what's right and best for them. When I talk about "passing the torch," I refer to passing on our knowledge and talents to others. Through writing this chapter I hope my children, in addition to my readers, will reap the benefits of what I've learned in life. I really would like my books to serve as shards of knowledge that others can use to cut through the confusion that life sometimes throws our way.

There is an interesting theory floating around that we human beings have the ability to draw accidents and illnesses into our lives. This theory may have some merit to it. I've learned through my dealings with the otherside that we have the ability to adjust our energy to benefit us, so on the flip side, is it possible to adjust our energy in a negative way and draw cancer or murder to us? Here's where I get hung up: I'm aware that human beings "sense" things and have premonitions of what will be, so is it possible to misread a prediction that makes us fearful as actually "drawing" a bad situation to us? To separate the two theories seems almost impossible to prove, but I'll try and let you be the judge.

From what I've learned from my own predictions, I know that I've been able to see a physical area in a person's body that needs to be scanned. Once scanned, it is determined that the person in question has the beginning stages of breast cancer. This is nothing she feared before, yet she has it. Did she draw it to her, as some might suggest? Do some things just happen because it's fate? Why was I able to see the problem area and predict illness in her chest? All of these are good questions that we should be able to answer.

I believe that most of the people who've died who I've brought through had sensed their own demise; sometimes they even say that they had always felt they'd die prematurely or knew around what time in their life they'd pass. I believe they had "feelings," intuition, even flashes of how they'd die, and they feared it. Who wouldn't? Most of us can't visualize ourselves growing old or even getting gray hair or wrinkles. In some readings the deceased mention that they knew that they were going to die young.

My friend Domini was one of those people. She wasn't a big worrywart; she was a go-with-the-flow kind of a person, so I think she's a good example. The first time Domini mentioned that she thought she'd die young was when she was around nineteen years old. That was when she made me promise that if anything ever happened to her I would take care of her baby girl. She was serious about this conversation and about her dying young, but she in no way seemed frightened at the prospect of death. A couple of years later I warned her that she needed to take better care of herself or she was going to die around the age of thirty.

I can safely rule out my prediction being why she passed away at thirty-one years old because I've also made predictions about other people's health and it saved their lives. I am sure that when people die it is not in my hands. I'm simply used as a tool to save or to warn and attempt to intervene on someone's behalf, and all I can do is give my information hoping that it helps.

I never saw Domini truly fear death until she was already diagnosed with inoperable cancer. That was the first time I had ever seen fear in my friend's eyes. I more than understood her fear, and it killed me not to be able to intervene for her and buy her time. It is my belief that the part of Domini that had always felt invincible came to terms with the part of her that knew she'd never live to be old when the diagnosis was handed down. She wasn't ready to go and fear started to resonate within her.

Unfortunately, I have no control over when someone dies, or I'd use it to take out sex offenders who victimize children—that'd be quite the talent. And I'd help preserve the people who deserve to live long lives because they're so necessary in our world. But then maybe I'd throw off a delicate balance that sustains us without us understanding why things have to play out the way they do. That's why it's not in my hands or yours.

Anyway, I learned an enormous lesson when I tried to prevent my dad's death by asking him to go get a checkup to keep his "ticker" healthy. I learned that even though I had a premonition involving my dad and knew he was going to pass at sixty-seven of a massive heart attack, I couldn't stop it. This taught me that his life was never in my hands. In addition, I never told my dad about my prediction, and I knew that he took great care of himself physically, so one couldn't make the argument that my prediction fed a fear that he had and drew death to him.

My dad didn't want to die. He loved life, but I had always sensed that he worried about his time being cut short. I have to make the argument that he personally had sensed early death his whole life and he had fought it with healthy eating and regular exercise. I believe this eliminates the argument that an overwhelming, sudden fear of death could send out a strong energy that would draw death to you. Two different girlfriends of my dad's told me that he had mentioned that he worried about dying prematurely throughout his life.

It is possible that owning the energy within you that believes or fears your death can cause your death to manifest physically, but if it's how your death was always going to unfold anyway, then didn't your "feeling" or worry simply contribute to fate? And is it possible that a healthy caution sign doesn't hurt us but could instead save us? Could my dad's lifelong fear of dying have made him more cautious with his health, which shows that he hadn't given in to dying young but rather was forcefully fighting off death? Could his fear have prolonged his life? If he had believed that ignoring his sense of dying young would save him, would he have taken his life for granted and not bothered taking care of his health? We'll never know, but what I do know is that my dad didn't take his life for granted and he did spend time making me laugh and he enjoyed looking good through his health regimen so, as he would say, "no regrets!"

Can a fear of dying in a car accident cause you to buckle your seat belt and in turn save your life? Can a fear of murder fuel you to learn self-defense or to be more safety conscious and avert dying at the hands of another? I have seen fear change people's lifestyles for the better because fear makes you look at what you have to lose if you don't pay attention to what's around you. Fear doesn't feel good, but neither do vaccinations. They are both necessary to protect us from harm. But if you let the fear consume your life, I believe it does manifest itself physically as a reaction to your constant drowning in negativity.

All-consuming fear really prevents you from living, anyway, and the reaction in your system is for your physical self to give in to your spiritual breakdown. I believe that it's possible to adjust your fear energetically by learning to identify the feeling that you get when you fear and then saying to yourself, "I'm going to take my fear and think of it as a road sign that's telling me what I need to do to be safe and take care of myself."

So the next time you feel fear, have some sort of mantra as a rebuttal to the fear. Your mantra (which is whatever makes you feel better) will counter the feeling of helplessness that fear brings up. It will give you some energetic say in the matter and therefore remove the feeling of "free falling" and replace it with a positive reaction that says to fear, "I hear you and I'm taking precautions to ensure my well-being."

The alternative argument that we draw to us what we fear is a possible contributing factor in our lives, but I don't believe that it's singularly responsible for our deaths or debt. There is a lot to be said for positive thinking or negative thoughts being a factor in our lives and how they turn out. Maybe we attract like energy to us and therefore we make no money because we surround ourselves with others who are going nowhere fast.

When you put energy out in the world, it either attracts or repels people who either vibe with you or don't. Philosophers surround themselves with like-minded people they can learn from. We're drawn to people in whom we see a similar energy thread to ourselves, or people whom we loved or once admired, and if they aren't good for us then we are placing ourselves in a vicious destructive cycle.

So is it possible to draw to you what you energetically put out in the world, meaning good finances, bad finances, love, no love, death, life? Yeah, I believe so. And I think it's important to point out that energy can be ever changing and can evolve in a positive way or fester with no movement or growth. So take a look at the people you surround yourself with and decide for yourself if you're where you want to be and with whom you want to keep company. Inventory your soul, if you will.

Do we fear what will be, or will it be what we fear? This is a case of which came first, the chicken or the egg? You be the judge of what feels right to you.

CHAPTER 6

Mirror, Mirror

A monumental lesson that I've learned from all of the readings I've done boils down to this: anyone's childhood will affect all the other generations around him or her, both living and dead. This is important to recognize because it will affect how well you live your life and ultimately how well you'll die. Children are a mirror image of somebody in the family, whether physically or in personality or both. Young people see and compare the similarities between themselves and others, so it's important to reflect the best parts of us for the younger family members so they too can live the best that they can. It's also important to teach young people the concept of living two or three lifetimes in one (I will explain this life strategy further). So this chapter attempts to get you to reflect on your

childhood. I'll reflect on my childhood and share stories from readings and show how those kids were affected as well as how they affected others.

I try in each of my books to be candid with my
readers and let them get to know my "real" family
and friends so that they have a snippet of the real
story of my life. I look back on my own past and
where I came from so that you might relate and do
the same. This is key in a person's life because our
childhood seems to be where some of us had to learn
to demand to be loved and the rest of us knew what
it was truly to be loved.

Some people might have a problem with my use
of the word "demand." What I mean is that we were
put in positions to have to self-search and figure out
what exactly made us feel loved and not settle for less
than that in life. It's okay not to settle in life just as
long as we reasonably recognize what is humanly
possible.

When I was four years old, there was a motorcycle
accident involving a young man off Thirty-second
Street where I grew up. I remember walking out to
the side of the road with my mom and picking up a
shoe. While my mom looked on and said a prayer for
the man, I buried his shoe on the side of the road. I
didn't know why, I just felt somehow I was showing
him respect.

Not until a few years ago did my mom tell me that

on the day of the accident we were at a gas station where the guy on the motorcycle was filling up his gas tank. She asked me if I remembered that. Honestly, I was hazy on that exact moment, but it sounded familiar. I was just so young then. My mom then told me that the man had died at the scene of the accident. That made sense to me inside, but as I concentrated trying to remember the little details of that day so long ago in 1976, the confirmation of his death saddened me greatly. I still wonder what instinct motivated me to try to bury his shoe. I had a sense that I was doing something good for the poor guy in the accident.

Children feel deeply and sometimes become adults who have developed defenses and learned how to put up walls because that's a natural human reaction to disappointment. My mom remembers all the details of the day the young man died, and I remember the "feelings" that I had that day as if it were yesterday.

I bring this up because many things can be absorbed from children, invaluable qualities that are precious and vital to learning how to emotionally touch others. Allowing us to learn that some people will honor our trust, we decide whether or not to show people who we really are and whether or not to trust anyone with our quirks and flaws.

Our quirks and flaws are the best part of our personalities. I have what some people see as a flaw (one of many), which is that I'm honest to a fault and very direct, sometimes too direct. I like that about me and I like that I'm not afraid to battle for what I believe is right. Write down your flaws and get rid of the ones that you really feel aren't good for you. Realize that the ones that make you smile are "good flaws" that enhance your personality. Celebrate them and stop apologizing for them!

While growing up, I realized at a very young age that keeping my mouth shut was somehow going to stop adults from getting madder at each other and maybe they'd quit fighting. Some people will relate to this. It took me until I was an adult to find my voice and to be assertive. I have gotten it down to a science now. It's important for me not to take it too far but rather remember that there are moments when it's time to be sensitive. If we can learn to take the best parts of us as children and incorporate them into who we are as grown-ups, I believe all of us can live incredibly happy, focused lives.

Make a list of things that you liked about yourself when you were young and days that were really happy—I mean the best. Some people will say that their list is short because they didn't have a great childhood; I say one or two items is all that you need. If in your childhood you always wanted to go to Disneyland and your parents never took you, go now, wear the mouse ears, ride the rides, and give yourself the moments you always wanted. I always wished that my parents had played with me in the pool when I was little. (Truthfully, I don't even know if my dad could swim because never once did I see him do so.) I take that childhood desire now that I'm a parent and I play Marco Polo in the pool with my kids, and we have handstand contests and water wars.

By doing this and passing these great memories on to my kids, I've filled my own small gap that I had inside. It wasn't that my parents did anything wrong. I simply took the "I wish when I was small . . ." energy that I still carried inside and turned it into something positive. The desire for that childhood experience is now gone because I addressed it and gave myself what I needed. As anyone can observe from the people they grew up with, we all carry inside of us the child we once were, and it's very fulfilling to give to yourself what a family member or friend didn't know you needed. I mean it. Make a list and you'll be shocked at how good it feels to take back your youth.

I loved Frankenberry, Count Chocula, Boo Berry, and Fruity Yummy Mummy cereals when I was small. I wasn't often allowed to have them, so when I was, I went overboard trying to eat the whole box of cereal. One day I happened to be in Culver City, California, and a painting caught my eye. I did a double take: the huge canvas painting had all four of my favorite childhood monster cereals represented larger than life. You know what I did? I bought the amazing Drizzle painting. It hangs in my bedroom, and every morning I wake up and look at it and I smile. Yeah, it came with an adult price tag, but it makes me feel like a little girl again, and that renews me. It's especially important because my job often makes me feel so old inside.

My girls love it and it makes them happy too. They'll all remember that their mom made life into an event and knew that there are few things in life that provide you with a feeling of healing inside. They'll remember that I never wavered when it came to making them feel loved. If it's that important to them, no matter what it is, then it's that important to me.

In my childhood I dealt with more serious topics than getting my favorite cereal, topics like multiple divorces and violence in the family. I also dealt with racial issues stemming from my dad's side of the family where some of my less than kind "family members" called me the "white sheep of the family" since they were Hispanic and I was half German. They're kind of dramatic women and I was a great topic of conversation, but I bet I'm a better topic for them at dinner now, don't you think?

Now, instead of focusing on my hurdles in childhood, I choose to embrace who I was inside as a kid and what made me happy because the same things still make me happy, and I expand on that. The way I have always looked at it is that someone always had it worse than me and everyone has his or her own cross to bear. I refuse to let my childhood be over-shadowed by the hard times. I remember when I was small, lying on my back in my front yard staring at the clouds and trying to figure out if they looked more like bunnies or cats. That was a healthy moment in childhood that many of us had. I do that with my girls now, and these are the kinds of memories that come through in readings from the deceased.

As grown-ups, there are times when we have to be ultraresponsible for bills, our children's well-being, our professions, health care for older members of our family (I know this one because I was financially re-sponsible for my grandma Jenee who has Parkinson's disease for a little over a year), and millions of other things. We become so bogged down in responsibili-ties that we lose ourselves to them. In my opinion, there needs to be a healthy marriage of both being responsible and renewing ourselves.

I incorporate the fun grown-up things I like to do, such as going out for three-hour dinners with friends, with juvenile fun stuff like riding the major roller coasters with Aurora. It was fun when I was eleven and it's still fun now, although I must admit I don't shake it off physically like I used to. Still, it's a blast because it makes Aurora giggle. When you truly want to know how to get the most out of your life, look to your childhood for some of your answers.

Now that I've shared part of my childhood with you, what do you remember doing that put a twinkle in your eyes? Please don't worry about what someone will think of you if you're fifty and go roller-skating or if you're seventy and buy a lollipop. You'll have a huge smile on your face and in your heart. Feeling good is contagious, and when I see people who are at an age where they normally wouldn't take part in certain activities, I stand by watching them be free, and by looking in their eyes, I can see what they looked like in their twenties because their soul projects it to the outside.

Looking good is a priority to many of us, and there are doctors to help us achieve our physical best, but I've noticed (and I think people will agree with me on this) that when a person no matter how old is "beaming" with joy, it shows on his or her face and takes years off how old he or she looks. It's up to us how well we want to live.

I'm cramming two or three lifetimes into my one because I want to *live*. I'm not only going to live a successful family life and be a great mom. I'm going to break barriers in my profession too and have fun socializing and meeting interesting people and learning from them as well. You just have to direct your energy to corners of your life that are deserving of your time and energy, and cut your losses in areas that don't pay off emotionally, spiritually, or even financially.

Don't spin your wheels and throw your time and energy down a bottomless pit, because that takes away from adding soul-building moments to your life. When you help someone or do something that is emotionally fulfilling to you, it strengthens your soul. You can actually feel a great satisfaction from within that puts a bounce in your step, and when that happens you know you've done something that sends out positive energy around you. Don't waste a day on bitterness or being a doormat. Teach those around you how to treat you and then teach them how to live well by example.

I need people to grasp the fact that although I have the ability to do some extraordinary things, I also hold dear the parts of my life that are ordinary. One of those ordinary yet valuable traits is that I'm a mom to three little girls. I love relating to other parents, especially now that our oldest is a teenager. Many people can understand where I'm coming from as a parent. The only difference is that I have a daughter who yells at me, and this is a direct quote, "Mom! I can't get away with anything! That's so unfair!"

Maybe it is unfair, but I thank God every day that I have my special antennae that can pick up on my daughter's friends' motives and half-truths. I think most moms have some of that special instinct that detects when you're being given a line of bull. Part of being a teenager is testing boundaries and trying to see what you can get away with. I've been there and it's just a part of life. So in order to try to understand someone who is seen as "unique" or "unusual," it's important to learn to appreciate both her strengths and her flaws. I have an unlimited supply of both. There, I said it—I'm not perfect, never claimed to be.

I have three daughters, Aurora, Fallon, and Sophia, who share my gift as well as my headaches in life. Besides that shared trait they are natural wonders to me, and I have savored every moment of their lives and will continue to do so. From the moment they were each born, I breathed in their beauty and innocence. I see parents who think of children as accessories or burdens, and I don't understand their blindness. I'm sure that many people share that feeling with me. I remember giving a reading to woman, and it stands out for me because I have never had a reading like hers before and I hope never to have one again. I saw that her son had passed and I told her that he wanted her to know that he was beautiful now. She looked annoyed and said, "My son was retarded. He was never beautiful. I want to hear about my finances."

She denied him while he was alive and she denied him after his death too. I was pretty shocked, and I disagree with her; I think that he was incredibly beautiful in life and death. I'm not sure if she knows how she came across, but she was downright icy. The young man who had just wanted his mom to be proud of him taught me that children are almost always better people than we are. That statement may shock some people, but I stand by it. Children are open, feeling beings, and love and hope reside in their eyes. There is nothing in the world that compares to looking into children's eyes and having them beam at you; you can see a glimpse of their vibrant soul. I will never forget that boy as long as I live. It comforts me to know that he's now with people who appreciate him, and now you care about him too and that no doubt makes him feel good.

Children can be challenging, but they're worth the challenge. I love it when one of my daughters repeats a nugget of wisdom that I once said to her or to one of her friends. I love it when they hang over my shoulder at Thanksgiving trying to learn how to make my green apple and chestnut stuffing. There is so much to love about children. I always hope that people realize it's never too late to learn to be a good parent or grandparent. I've noticed that kids can be quite forgiving when it comes to their parents, even grown kids. In your life you have moments when you hold someone's heart in your hands, and I hope my asking people to live better lives encourages them to love big.

When I work a case, each victim, especially the small ones, becomes my own family. This is not because I am forced or asked to feel this way but because every victim is a soul worth connecting with. I take it personally when a child is raped or killed—we all should. I know that living the way I do seems like a liability, but really I've opened myself up to the wounded, and their eyes return all the energy I give to them. They return it to me through the moments I spend with them when their eyes forget to hold fear as they look at me. I know that those who've been severely wounded carry a look in their eyes as though they're dead inside. For them to let go of the fear even for a moment there has to be an instinctive trust within them for me, and I honor that trust.

I've met many victims of violent crimes, and they all matter to me. I recently met a little girl who was five and had been kidnapped and sexually assaulted by a stranger. I will never forget her face. Her eyes had a look in them that no child should ever have. I didn't want to leave her. Joe jokes that our house would be overflowing if I were permitted to keep all these children in an attempt to protect them. So I help put away the people who are responsible for making these kids feel fear on such high levels, the people who are the real bogeymen in our society. It's my attempt to protect the victims before they are victimized so that they never have the look in their eyes that replaces their innocence.

People often ask me whether if I see a crime coming I do something to prevent it. What I think people don't realize is that helping to put away criminals is my way of helping to prevent a future crime, because I assure you there is a potential victim walking the streets at any given time of the day. For the record, I've had the opportunity to work around some of the most violent, soulless criminals who breathe, and let me tell you, all they're waiting for is an opportunity to get away with another violent crime. So be safe and be smart. Children can be affected for the rest of their lives by adults.

Maybe by bringing up the topic of kids, my readers will hug their children more or notice the lonely child next door who is always ignored and maybe your kids can share some kindness with him. That's how you begin to build your soul up to levels that will put you at the top of the human race. I assure you that taking the time to reach out to children around you is something you'll never regret.

Parents who have lost children should know that they take with them the sparkling moments that you shared with them in life. They always worry more about their parents than themselves, and I never get tired of the drawings they show me or the plays they were in or the meals they loved when they were alive. We are all connected, and living children as well as children who "live again" tell me what matters to them the most. It is a strong sign of trust. I collect their memories and laughter, learning spiritually from them all.

CHAPTER 7

It's All Perspective

*P*eople sometimes don't realize that I have bad days too, days that involve self-pity and being quite human. Really, we all do have these bad days. Sometimes our moments of self-pity can be remedied by interaction with another person who inspires and reminds us of the importance of appreciating the life that we have.

Joe was in the office shuffling papers and I was looking in the mirror staring at the smile lines that no longer leave my face when I have stopped smiling. Some of you can relate to what I'm saying. Anyway, the TV was on and I heard a female voice talking. I was distracted by the young voice long enough to stop wallowing in self-pity and to walk into the bedroom to see who it was. On the screen was a seventeen-year-old girl who had an unmistakable look in her eyes that announced that she had seen and thought things that many grown-ups hadn't. She'd experienced life in "fast-forward." I sat on the edge of the bed and turned up the volume. She was sharing a story of young courage and even of joy. This may sound strange after I fill you in on the details of the girl's life. She had terminal cancer and knew what that entailed, inevitable death. Yet she looked happy and proud of her journey in life so far. Some would ask, "How can that be?"

Her story already was inspiring, and it became more inspiring when she mentioned that the Make-A-Wish Foundation had granted her last wish. She had a high school sweetheart she wanted to marry before she died. So the Make-A-Wish Foundation, one of my favorite and in my opinion most valuable foundations in the world, had created a fairy tale wedding just for her. I found myself mesmerized by the girl who stood before us in her cascading white gown as she beamed with certain happiness. I say that because she knew that her wedding day was to be savored right now and not muddied by what lay ahead of her. She wasn't saying, "Why me?" like most of us naturally would, but rather she spoke of nothing but her gratitude for all who supported her in her life.

At that moment it resonated in my soul that she

would never have the luxury of growing old enough to complain about something as trivial as wrinkles, as I just had. That thought alone could have put life back into perspective for me. My mind chose to take it further, thinking that this girl would never be able to complain about her kids riding her motherly nerves or her husband spending too much time at the office. There would be no complaints about not getting the job she wanted or having to take an extra class to graduate from college due to changed guidelines. I tell people that when you're feeling down, you can always look around and learn how to bring yourself up again.

I thought this story was important to share with you because I know how precious life is, and I get into a slump from time to time. It's okay, it's human, but when you have these moments it is crucial to open your eyes and take a good look around you. I opened my eyes that day, and it was like getting an adjustment to my soul that realigned it. Life never ceases to astound me. The person we need to teach us a lesson somehow appears when we need him or her the most.

Later that week I was out to dinner with Joe and some friends. One of our friends was feeling in the gutter about his age. I didn't give him the old, "There are people worse off than you are," because the moment didn't warrant it, and that never seems to help anyway. We all heard it from our moms often enough to render the meaning powerless, even though it's true.

I said, "Do you know that there will always be someone who would gladly change places with you? I mean, if you're forty, then someone fifty would gladly accept ten years of antiaging relief. If you're seventy, there's someone eighty who thinks you're still a kid. It's all perspective."

This thought alone has really adjusted my way of thinking as far as reminding me to live in the now yet plan for the future. I'm quite sure that I'm not the only person who was inspired by the seventeen-year-old girl, but I hope that by sharing her story I can cast her message even further. A *big* thank-you to her family for having such a magnificent girl to share with us all. Their little angel has left a big impression through sharing her life with others.

People often ask me, "Why do bad things happen to good people?" Think about it. With just one interview, the teenager snapped the rest of us into line spiritually as she inspired countless numbers of people to live life with gratitude and conviction. So although it would be a utopia if no one good ever died, we need to be reminded that we have the potential to live a great life and to work together to move ourselves forward spiritually and otherwise. If a rotten person dies, not many pay attention because he's an uninspiring person who only teaches us how *not* to be in life.

AMBER

It's very important to Joe and me to pass on the lessons we learn in life to Aurora, Fallon, and Sophia. I had been humbled and moved by the seventeen-year-old girl I just spoke of, and I wanted our girls to share the same sort of growth experience. I'm well aware that these moments make us more empathetic people. That in turn strengthens our souls and opens our hearts and minds, which is the whole point of our being "feeling" creatures.

The opportunity presented itself on November 30, 2006. I was at home listening to Johnjay and Rich on KISS-FM fulfilling Christmas wishes for deserving people. One wish was for a woman named Susie and her five-year-old daughter Amber. The little girl was in the hospital being treated for leukemia; she had been in remission but no longer was.

I stopped what I was doing and perched on my bed to listen more carefully to their story. In the background you could hear Amber, and her little voice moved me to tears. I love the age where a child's voice still sounds a little bit like a baby, real high-pitched, yet she can communicate far better. Upon hearing that she was about to receive items that would make her life much easier, the mom began to cry. She was given an unlimited cell phone for a full year so that she could communicate with her other kids who were out of state staying with family members. You can imagine how important that would be to a mother. Paying a phone bill was stressful and no doubt weighed heavily on her. She couldn't work because she cared for her daughter in the hospital twenty-four hours a day, seven days a week. There were toys for Amber and clothes for both of them and much, much more. When the mom heard of the gifts, her first response was, "I can't accept them; there's someone out there who needs them more."

Can you believe that? What a selfless and innocent thing to say.

Johnjay and Rich insisted and she relented, graciously accepting the kind gifts.

I knew that I had to meet this little girl and her mother. That very day I went shopping for this precious little girl with my friend Jen. I found turquoise pajamas with funny little roosters all over them and doll-making kits and card games to help them pass the time. I wrapped these and other gifts beautifully in Christmas paper and mentally prepared myself for the special meeting. I was filled with great energy anticipating meeting this little girl.

Joe contacted the woman who had set up the radio interview and arranged for us to meet the family. I told Fallon and Sophia about Amber, and they were glad to be meeting with her too. (Aurora had cheer practice, so I'd have to share a growth moment with her another time. Pulling a teenager away from what she loves to do is like pulling her teeth out without painkillers. Now was not the time for dentistry, so I would have to impact her in another way at a later time.) I told my girls a little about Amber's illness so that they could better understand why she was in the hospital. I told them that her blood was "sick" and the doctors were going to give her some stronger blood to try to make her well. I'm no doctor, but I did the best I could.

The next day rolled around, and Joe and I picked up our two youngest girls from school early to go to the hospital and meet Amber. Joe spoke with Susie, and she told him that Amber was finishing up five hours of treatment. I can't even imagine watching your baby go through that. The parents must have to find such courage within themselves to endure their child's pain, as I'm sure they feel for her on every level. I'm convinced that when you love someone that much you are forced to find the courage in the love that you have for her. You have no choice but to put her needs first.

We arrived at the hospital with our nine- and seven-year-old daughters, and they saw balloons and made a beeline for the gift shop. We settled on a stuffed pink reindeer and a teddy bear. They were adorable and colorful; we were sure they'd be welcome additions to Amber's bed. The stuffed animals had to be run through a hot dryer to remove germs, but the books and stuff didn't require that. This was good because I don't think the paper products would have made it out alive. Whew!

As many people are aware, hospitals are tough for me to endure, so I took a deep breath as I stepped into the elevator. My girls were chirping with excitement and I was very proud of them. They are compassionate, wonderful girls and I'm lucky to be their mom. We stepped out of the elevator and onto the children's ward. We were escorted into a changing area. Joe and I suited up in our hospital gowns and our girls had face masks and gowns with little Disney characters peppered on them.

We entered the room with gifts in hand, and Amber's little face lit up. This rendered us helpless but to return the smile. I noticed that Amber's hair was missing due to the radiation. I also noticed that Susie had shaved her own head to match her daughter's. Amber was missing some teeth since the doctor had to pull them for her protection so she didn't accidentally swallow a baby tooth. She still looked like a darling five-year-old girl with piercing brown eyes.

I hugged Susie, who told me that she didn't believe that we were really coming and that she was so happy to see us. I hugged Amber, and we watched her open her presents one by one. And since Susie is a fan of *Medium*, I presented her with an autographed copy of my DVD set from Season 1. We visited for a while, and then we said our good-byes so that Amber could rest. I told Amber that I would be checking in on her, and she looked especially happy to know that our girls would be back to visit her. I'm sure that when you see adults all day, it's nice to see others who come from Planet Kid. The Christmas spirit felt great; Amber loved her toys and Susie liked her gifts as well. Susie tried to turn down our Christmas mad money but I wasn't having that, so it was a battle of the wills.

Amber and her mom were both so uplifting to be around. It says a lot about people's soul/energy when they can be in such a complex, frightening situation and still have the spiritual strength to be invigorating to others. We headed out with full hearts and a little tired but sure that we'd see them again.

I shared this story because I was touched by a little girl's voice who reminded me of my own little girls, and I think that demonstrates how as human beings we can feel a connection with another person just by hearing his or her voice. I will always feel a connection to Amber, and she's a permanent guest in our family's hearts.

Many people are touched by others yet never let them know how much they have helped to enrich their lives. They say, "I'll tell them later." What people seem to miss is that sometimes there is no later, sometimes the person who touched you really needed to know that he or she was appreciated by you and that you noticed his or her efforts. Let people connect with you—there's a lot of love to be had by everyone and a lot of words that need to be said.

Don't let people who do the wrong thing become the focus. I believe that most people are good, and there's always going to be bad too because every coin has two sides to it; the sides cannot be separated. Try to be the good side. I know that "no good deed goes unpunished," but that is the chance we take to be able to do the right thing. I truly believe that one way or another, the wrongs will be made right eventually. People who are bad have nothing to lose and practically nothing to gain. Those who are good stand to lose their heart, their time, and sometimes their money, but they have everything to gain. So much more than they could ever possibly lose because you could never take a good person's soul or the fond memories that people have of him or her.

People who don't care about the sick or dying have already lost themselves. I don't mean that they need to single-handedly save the world, but a kind thought or a prayer for those in need does wonders and speaks volumes. Amber helped to show my daughters that people need each other and that being there for others bonds you. It also opens your eyes and in turn opens your heart, allowing you to grow into a pretty nice person. So, thank you Amber and Susie for sharing your life with us. A special thank-you to the staff at the Phoenix Children's Hospital for taking exceptional and loving care of Amber.

One month later we had additional proof of how this little girl has touched so many. I had agreed to accompany Johnjay and Rich to Tucson for their Christmas Wish fund-raiser since I now had a vested interest in their charity as well as a boatload of Christmas spirit. We were still monitoring Amber's progress, since by this time she had received her bone marrow transplant, and it was now a waiting game to see if the transplant would be successful. She would either be cured or she would die; there was no in between.

Joe and I had taken a short break from the fund-raiser, as it had been a few hours since we started signing autographs and all that fun stuff. During our break, Joe's phone rang. It was Susie, who told Joe that Amber wasn't doing very well and to please pray for her. This impacted me in a big way since we were in Tucson to raise money for the Christmas Wish program, the same program during which I first heard Amber's little voice. Now here we were hearing from Susie about the girl we had grown so attached to in such a short time. The news was devastating, and Joe and I exchanged looks of fear and helplessness.

Joe and I had to return to the show to help raise more funds, and as Johnjay and Rich concluded the show that had run for twelve hours that day, I made an on-air request. I asked the listeners to pray for Amber. To pray that she be given enough strength and protection to make it through. I believe energy and prayers—especially mass prayers—are high energy being focused for the same purpose, and that is strong and in this case necessary. I hoped that if enough of us cared, maybe we could pull Amber back to us. My voice was shaky as I tried to encourage people to help grant the most important Christmas Wish of all that night. I wanted to give Amber the best possible chance to win her battle and to let her know that people cared about her.

I was in the studio with JohnJay and Rich, plus microphones, headsets, and a big viewing window that made me feel like a goldfish in a bowl. As I tried to pull myself together, I'd get moved right back to tears looking at the crying eyes of the audience. Mothers were hugging their children, people were praying, and Amber was being loved in that moment by tens of thousands of people who cared. It was an organic, moving moment that just happened, and it truly represented the season of caring.

Joe and I went next door to meet our friend Randy for a cup of Christmas cheer and I was emotionally drained. It was a little Irish pub that I'd never been to before. It was right out of the 1960s and I loved it. I decided to play a song on the jukebox and something directed me to Willie Nelson. I glanced over the songs, and one stood out in particular that I knew was meant to be played for Amber. It was a song that I'd never heard before, titled "Angel Flying Too Close to the Ground." As I listened to the lyrics, I hoped that the mass prayer would be enough to tilt the odds in that little angel's favor. I again hung my head low and I prayed with everything I had within me.

We checked in with Susie every few days to monitor Amber's progress, and a few weeks later we received the news that Amber had steadily improved and that the doctors were cautiously optimistic for her. I know that the prayers helped, and I'm positive that all of the strangers who loved her like their own that night took part in raising her up too high to pull to the ground. The last time we talked to Susie, Amber was doing just fine.

I've always been reminded by the otherside that miracles do happen and that sometimes children are our angels on earth and they teach us to care about others more than ourselves.

On a lighter note, speaking of life throwing us curves and the importance of living every day to its fullest, I want to share with you some of the fun experiences that I had this year. Most of my readers know that I have a list of "things to do before I die" and every year I cross off a few items after accomplishing them. I share these with you to inspire you to write your own list as well as to remind people that it doesn't matter how small the life moment is on your list; if it makes you giddy, it's a big deal.

One of my favorite moments was on a trip to Denver for our friends Andrea and Dustin's wedding. Joe and I were with my friend/assistant Jen and her husband, Aaron. We were meeting two other friends of ours for the wedding as well. Some of you might know them: Adrianne Curry, the first winner of *America's Next Top Model*, and Chris Knight, Peter Brady from *The Brady Bunch*, who star in their reality show,

My Fair Brady on VH-1. Both are wonderful people and have become very good friends of ours.

We were staying at a beautiful resort in Colorado Springs, having the time of our lives being silly and somewhat immature. We were returning from Andrea and Dustin's get-together the night before their wedding. When we got back to the hotel, I walked through the automatic doors at the entrance. The six of us were going to have a nightcap and retire for the night. I had a nagging desire to window-shop at the gift store, and as I approached it I could see a young bride and her groom taking pictures outside of their reception hall.

Anyone who's read my books knows that I'm a bit of a child inside. On my list of things to do in my life, I have some serious tasks and some that are purely for fun, which is great too. Well, this moment fell under "fun." I had always wanted to crash a wedding. Yeah, I know it's immature, but if you take yourself too seriously in life you might as well pack it in. As the smile on my face grew wider, I noticed the sign outside of the reception and it read "Knight Wedding." What a coincidence—I had my friend Chris Knight with me. Joe looked at me and said, "Allison, what's going through that head of yours?"

My excitement took over and I approached the couple, letting them know that I had a friend with their same last name who was also staying at the hotel. I mean, what were the chances? I'd never even been to Colorado Springs or that resort before. They were Knights, so I decided that this was the wedding for me. The couple looked unsure of why I was telling them this. I thought to myself, "Wouldn't Chris and Adrianne's presence give these kids a great story to tell their grandchildren?"

I did it! I dropped their names like a shameless plug, knowing that most everyone who hasn't been living under a rock remembers the '70s teen idol Christopher Knight, aka Peter Brady. They looked at me like I was playing a mean trick on them, but I wasn't and I intended to seal this deal. I told them I'd be right back. Chris was a little annoyed with me, but Adrianne responded to my idea of how special it would be for this couple to have a great wedding story for years to come.

When we rounded the corner walking toward the newly married couple, their eyes grew wide and their jaws dropped. Adrianne and Chris were a class act and agreed to pose for pictures with the couple.

While they did that, Joe and I slipped into the reception hall to do a little dancing, and I picked up a beautiful strawberry and dipped it in the cascading chocolate fountain. This was a truly memorable moment for me as well as for the young couple. They had successfully talked Adrianne and Chris into entering the reception hall to meet some of their guests. Chris cast me some daggers as I grinned and waved to him. He was kidding around and could see that the newlyweds and their families were very nice people. I had to dance to fully feel the moment, and Joe and I talked to several guests as they swooned over Chris's charisma and good looks as well as Adrianne's beauty and generous spirit. Joe and I felt lucky to have such impulsive friends, and boy were they good sports! Chris threatened to tell them who Joe and I were and I shook my finger at him jokingly and told him to stop being so mean. Well, those weren't my exact words, but I'm sure that you can guess what my exact words might have been. Well, surprise! I guess they'll know who we are now.

We all slipped out to have that nightcap and I thanked Chris and Adrianne for being with me as I crossed off one of my favorite life list challenges. I had wanted to crash a wedding for years and now I was totally happy with my accomplishment. We had showed up at the end of their reception when two-thirds of the guests had already left. It's a good thing the couple has pictures to prove that incident really happened, or who would believe their story? (I heard that the pictures have been posted on the internet, and who can blame them?)

Remember, everyone's list will be different, and that's good; variety makes life more interesting.

Maybe you would like to learn a foreign language or how to play an instrument that you've always wanted to master. For others it can be rolling down a hill of clover in Ireland. Oh, actually that's on *my* list!

People often share their list with me, and it makes me feel good knowing there are people out there with the desire to make the most of their life. These people understand that this is not a dress rehearsal. Many of us can get so caught up in what others think that we make ourselves unhappy. Some might not understand why crashing a wedding reception was so much fun, but I loved it. What makes you giddy? When was the last time you had a good belly laugh? Be different, but more important, be happy with your life and how you spend your time.

The day after crashing the Knight wedding, I attended a wedding that I was actually invited to, for our friends Andrea and Dustin. Their wedding was storybook beautiful and we enjoyed every minute of it. Thank you to both couples for sharing your special day with Joe and me. I'm a hopeless romantic, and weddings are the crescendo of romance. As my dad always said, "Live life large and make no apologies for who you are!" So there you go, great advice to inspire you to go make your own list of things you want to do with your time in life. If you're not having the time of your life, take a second look at how you've spent your days so far and then decide how you can make the rest of your life unforgettable.

The deceased often show me their wedding day as one of the happiest days of their lives even if the marriage didn't last. What we can learn from that is that our lives are peppered with life-changing moments that don't need to be judged as a whole but rather day by day. There may be some years in your life that were happier than others, but the fact that you had happy, memorable days at all says you've been blessed. The dead don't come through complaining about the bad times. They come through effervescent and so very grateful for and focused on the good times. That makes a lot of sense to me.

CHAPTER 8

Coping with the Loss of a Parent and Learning How to Reconnect with the Dead

WHAT HAVE I LEARNED SINCE LOSING MY DAD?

People ask me how I move forward every day after losing my dad, because anyone who's lost a parent knows how debilitating it can be. I lost my father to a heart attack, and I still call his phone number four years later hoping and waiting for him to answer. I know that he won't, but it feels good to push those numbers again. I can't bring him back, but all children who read this understand that I search myself for him. My eyes, my laugh, a bad joke remind me of him, which I love. Christina Aguilera's song "Hurt" conveys the sentiment felt by most people who have lost a loved one: "If I had just one more chance I would say how much I've missed you since you went away." But we can say it, they can hear us and, more important, they "feel" for us.

Every parent who's died hears us and feels us where he or she is, and I hope that anyone who's lost someone special really takes that to heart. Anyone who's lost a parent or will lose one will understand that this is a unique loss. Parents were the first to hold us when we were born, the first to love us, and the first people we loved. When you lose a parent, you feel like you might as well be five years old again, similar to when you got separated from your mom in a store, that sort of panic as well as the sick feeling in your stomach. Then you were reunited and all was right with the world again.

Death isn't so different. When you lose a parent, a panic kicks in and a sickness in your stomach rises, except we have to wait longer to be reunited with our parents in this case. But it will happen.

We seem instantly to place blame on ourselves as children, and this is the same no matter how old we get. I shoulda, coulda, woulda will not help you to understand why it was your loved one's time, so take a deep breath and physically let go of the guilt, exhale. Some of us, no matter how much we accomplish, can never fill the hole left by the "great one" in our life. You can't fill a bottomless pit with awards or money, and you shouldn't. I remember saying to Joe after the loss of my own dad, "No matter how much I accomplish or how successful I get, I can't bring my dad back."

I have a theory. In many of our childhoods we're taught that if we're really, really good we'll be rewarded and our parents will shower us with love and praise for our accomplishments. So when any of us lose someone to death, we're often reduced to being a child again emotionally. Our need to be with those we've loved and lost causes us to overachieve out of the desperate hope that a higher power will reward us with the return of our loved one.

I've seen so many highly successful people who were fueled by their pain from a loss and created financial empires out of their pain. The upside is there was a positive use of the pain that created something important that might not have been created otherwise.

The downside is that the person who built that empire from pain isn't healing inside and this is preventing him or her from reconnecting with the loved one.

I want to help these people first to recognize that they are still harboring the pain and then give some healthy suggestions to help them work through it. Why is it important to work through it? Because if you carry the pain inside it can manifest into other things, such as a serious physical illness, and it also will rob you of enjoying the rest of your life. There is a healthy amount of pain that you can carry without it taking over your life.

I'll be the guinea pig. I still miss the way it was when my dad was alive and I could hug him and watch him play with my kids. But I also know that he watches over my kids out of love as well as protection. I can't hug him, but I can remember what it felt like when he hugged me, so that feeds me emotionally. This is a healthy way for me to work on processing the pain that I carry from his loss, and anyone can apply this thinking to his or her own situation.

The more frequently I adjust my pain in exercises such as this one, the more I can feel the pain that literally can eat a person up from the inside out disappear from my body. When I miss going to the movies with my dad, I take my kids to the same theater that he took me to when I was small. We get a big bucket of popcorn and I insist on extra butter for it just like he and I always did. My girls and I sit and talk about their favorite memories of Grandpa Mike, and we belly-laugh because my dad was really funny.

After writing the sentence about my dad taking me to the movies at a particular movie theater, I received an invitation to a social gathering. At this party I met a man by the name of Dan Harkins, whose dad had owned a string of Harkins Theaters, including the one that my dad and I frequented, which is also the one Joe and I take our girls to. I was thrilled to meet him, and he was an extremely nice man with a lively tie.

I told him how many great memories I had with my dad at his family theaters and I thanked him. When I told him the one that was my favorite, he paused and said, "Well, we're not publicizing this, but that theater is closing." Obviously I was a little sad, since most of the places my dad had taken me to throughout my life were now closed. He asked me if our family would like to come see a movie that weekend, and I knew that there was no way that I'd miss that one last time. Mind you, the gathering took place three days before the doors would close forever on that particular theater. Dan offered to set up a tour for my family so that I could say good-bye, and I gratefully accepted.

We decided to go on Saturday since that was the day that my dad had always picked me up from my mom's when I was a kid for our weekend movie. We let Fallon pick the movie and she picked *Meet the Robinsons*. We made sure that our popcorn had extra butter and we found just the right seats and I glanced at our girls' smiling faces, thinking of how my dad must have done the same with me when I was little, taking in the sunshine that children exude when they're happy.

The previews started, and I was taken aback that a Mickey Mouse cartoon was being shown. You know, one of those three-minute cartoons that you never see before the feature film anymore but that used to be regular practice years ago. I looked at the Roman numerals at the bottom of the screen. The cartoon was made in 1983, some of my happiest days with my dad at this theater. I knew that I had seen that cartoon with my dad before.

The movie started, and the premise was a boy learning lessons about letting go of the past and embracing his future. He was also learning how being different from others is a good thing—it's what makes you, you. It really was a touching movie, and it had an animated frog called Franky who was sort of a frog mobster, and those characters reminded me of a picture hanging in our media room of the Rat Pack standing in front of the Sands hotel in Las Vegas back in the day. My dad loved orchestra music—the kind they played in the real happening clubs in the fifties—and my dad was very cool like the Rat Pack, so I thought of him. I laughed pretty loudly during that part of the movie.

At the end, the boy has to choose whether to live in the past or go forward, and when the words "Keep Moving Forward" flashed across the screen, I felt as though my dad was talking directly to me. We stayed a couple of extra minutes and I took a picture of our girls with Joe in their movie seats, and I really took in those last moments saying good-bye to a part of my childhood as well as a part of my girls' childhood. I will be forever grateful that the theater was there long enough for them to have their own memories there.

I have no doubt that my dad orchestrated my being at the soiree that Dan happened to be at, and it turns out that Dan and his wife had come to meet me because they saw my name on the guest list. How flattering is that? The timing was special. Had it been a week later, it would have been devastating to me, and if it was too much earlier the timing wouldn't have seemed as significant. My dad arranged a series of events so that I could say good-bye to a place that I held so special and to allow me to start looking forward instead of pining for the past and the way it used to be. Message received, Dad.

I'm teaching my girls how to process loss as well as how to reconnect with their granddad, and this is an example of what I mean when I say, "passing the torch." I'm passing to them the tools that will help them throughout their lives as well as tools that they will pass to their own children someday, tools that will help them when Joe and I die. I am showing them that our physical selves and our spiritual selves affect each other directly.

After our upbeat Grandpa Mike exercises, we take inventory of how we "feel" afterward and we listen carefully to our inner selves. This is such a healthy way to help children through loss. Participating in it with them strengthens your bond with them as well as your bond with those who've died, so it's win-win. It's important to teach children that it's okay to talk about people who've died and that it's quite all right to still talk to those who've passed on. Let young people know that your home is a safe place for them to talk freely about life and death. You'll be amazed at what kids will tell you once they know they can trust you, and this extends beyond their dreams and encounters with spirits.

Those of us who want to spend more time with those we feel we've lost just need to look in the mirror, because they were there all along. So how do we see past the tears? It's a matter of adjusting our perspective on death and learning how to stay connected to those that we love. Most people can no longer see those who've died by looking at them with their eyes. Rather, they have to learn to see them through their soul. What I mean by this is that you have to learn to connect with them through energies such as memories you have of them, especially songs. When you press the button to select that special song, you are energetically pressing a button that in a sense brings a particular deceased loved one to you because you've "requested" him or her. Music triggers the brain to remember times that you listened to that song before and in turn resurrects the way you felt in the past. Songs that are mutually special put you on the same energy "page" as the person you're missing. Music soothes the soul in many ways, and it's a powerful way to reconnect with those you love. The vibration of the music seems to be felt by both the living and those who live again.

When you're feeling intense emotions for the person who died, he is drawn to you because he knows he has your attention even if it's only through memories. When you allow yourself to connect to the soul of your loved one, it's a very powerful feeling. This is true in both life and death; the connection of both your energies just has to be redefined, that's all.

It takes practice and exercise to get used to flexing that part of your inner self, and it comes more easily for some because they've always had a grip on their understanding of their inner self and have a very healthy balance spiritually. If it doesn't come easily, don't give up. Keep trying. I'm a medium, and yet it took me losing my dad before I fully tried to reach beyond my physical self with everything that I had within me. This is not always easy, but I had a strong need to connect with him on his energetic terms.

Pain is a motivating factor that causes you to reconsider your belief system as well as a reason to do some serious inner reflection on who you are and what matters the most to you. People who refuse to acknowledge this natural reaction to death often shut down emotionally and become isolated and disconnected. In a way, they've "died" inside, but it's important for them eventually to decide to live again. It's important for your physical well-being to let your soul work through the pain, and it's core that your mind, body, and soul be equally exercised. Once you find yourself in this position, you are far more easily accessed by the otherside and you will find that your life starts making sense to you again.

When people have an imbalance within themselves, it acts as a rippling effect through every aspect of their life. You balance your mind, body, and spirit and all aspects of your life, whether it is your career, personal life, personal contentment. Whatever you see as important to your personal happiness will unfold effortlessly and with clarity. Rough spots in life serve a purpose too, because we're forced to learn from the hard times. Just be sure that if you're creating the drama in your life, you recognize that you need to break your cycle. Life is much easier when you get over yourself.

I've talked about connecting with the energy of those who've passed on and our need to learn from their successes and mistakes in order to live well. I also want to help you to understand that our loved ones are not trying to pass a soulful torch to us to further our attainments of material things. They lend us their power to push us forward in whatever it is that we want to do in life. Sometimes money comes attached to our accomplishments. That is fine, but it's not what motivates our loved ones to lend their power to us, because it is unimportant to them. There are some occasions where we stress over paying a bill, and many people have experienced a check or a refund of some sort coming in the mail for the exact amount they needed. Our loved ones feel the stress that causes us to feel depressed or unhappy, and they will often make sure that we have what we need when we need it the most. But it's not because the money is important to them—it's our emotional well-being that they care about.

Our deceased loved ones help us in various ways, especially when it has to do with family. If being the best parent you can be is your passion, then they come through to you and adjust your sense of awareness around your children. Souls are made of energy, so adjusting our energy is not hard for them to assist, or they can calm us with an energy wave of understanding for our child when we're at the end of our patience. We've all heard of someone who has "calming energy." Well, once the body is gone, that soul still has the capacity to calm others. Our personality traits are not gone once our body is no longer a part of us. Our humor, sarcasm, sweetness, or whatever we are inside is attached to our soul. If you want to have a successful business, then those who guide you from the otherside access your mind and help out with a sudden fresh idea or help you to meet the person who will help you in your business endeavors.

We can't even begin to imagine how often and in how many different ways those we love touch us daily. Recently Joe and I went back to one of my dad's favorite Mexican restaurants where I hadn't been able to eat because it held too many memories. It took me four and a half years to feel strong enough to take my kids there. On this particular day I was a little stressed because a really important interview had aired the day prior, so although it was a life-changing opportunity, I needed to decompress. My dad always used to cheer me up by saying something that would cause me to roll my eyes and say, "Daaaad, that's so corny!"

After we were seated and had ordered, Joe looked at me and said, "Goody gumdrops!"

I inquired, "Why did you say that?"

Joe said, "I don't know."

I was taken aback because my dad used to say those same words to me. I hadn't heard them in years and, frankly, I didn't think that I'd ever hear them again.

"Joe, my dad used to say that to me when he'd get excited about going out to lunch or seeing a movie, and I would roll my eyes like you wouldn't believe."

Those words were so unlike Joe ever to say, I mean *ever*!

I know that my dad put those words in Joe's head, and I know my dad used that opportunity to let me know that he was around me. It was particularly important to me on that day since just the night before I had wondered if he saw me accomplish the interview of a lifetime. I believe that I got my answer. I know that I feel better knowing there are caring souls looking out for my family. I find it reassuring rather than spooky that we're guided and watched over. After all, one day we'll be doing the guiding and watching for someone we love.

If I hadn't been an open-minded person, I would have just dismissed that occurrence as "strange" and missed out on being touched by my dad. It's not that our loved ones don't try to reach us through other people or signs. It's that pragmatic people tend to dismiss what they can't prove. You can be intelligent and still have a tight grasp on your spirituality. People who exercise only their mind and ignore their body and spirit find an imbalance in their life.

We've all met people who seemed kind of "vacant" inside and seemed to lack emotions or feelings. They are perplexing creatures, and there's nothing inside them to connect to because they don't feel comfortable connecting on emotional levels. It's really not a healthy way to be. We've also all met people who are completely spiritual and seem to lack grounding or an ability to think things through because they get agitated with those sort of details and would rather leave it all up to a higher power. There are also people who focus only on their physical strengths. These people are hard to grasp emotionally since they don't feel it's their strong suit and they are used to getting what they want with their looks.

There is a way to balance mind, body, and spirit and be comfortable with yourself on all three levels. You can be attractive, emotionally available, and have a good hold on common sense. There are many, many people who do a fine job at keeping themselves in check on all levels, and we call them successful and well-rounded. Some days you're going to feel a little off on one or more of your levels, and that's okay. It gives you an opportunity to reevaluate yourself.

CHAPTER 9

The Power of the Otherside

*P*eople often ask me about faith and what the deceased are able to make happen from the otherside. There are two stories that I want to share with you. They are two separate readings that took place within two days of one another, and both changed my life.

The first involved a missing nineteen-year-old girl named Jackie Hartman who disappeared January 28, 2007. She was last seen at a convenience store/gas station in Gilbert, Arizona, getting into a car with a young man she was going on a "date" with. Jackie's father confronted the young man the next day, who told him that Jackie had been dropped off alive.

I was contacted by a friend of her family and asked

to give my impressions around Jackie's disappearance. I agreed to do so, knowing that Jackie must have gone to great lengths to bring me in on her case. For one, I wasn't willing to take on a new case at that time. I also have a rule that if the suspect or perpetrator of the crime is in custody, I won't work the case. There are so many murders that I choose to work only on ones where the killer's still at large and finding him or her could save a life. I have to draw the line somewhere, because I'm only one person, and preventing a future crime has to be my motivation in working the case.

So circumstances took me beyond two of the hurdles that I had put up, but the clincher for me was Jackie's dad. I saw him on the news and he had so much love in his eyes for his daughter and I could feel his heart break. I could feel the lump in his throat, but most important, I "felt" his urgency and unyielding determination to bring his daughter home even if only to lay her to rest. I also wanted whoever was behind the crime to have thirty million people see his face on television and have them know what he did and who he was. I thought of it as a little justice for Jackie and her family, and I knew from the time that I saw Jackie's face on the evening news that somehow I would work her case. I'm stubborn, but when it's right, it's right, and I at least would be able to tell Jackie's dad when his little girl would be brought home.

This case was unlike any other that I had worked because it involved letting a camera crew follow me to document my information for a television show. On Monday, February 5, I went to visit the crime scenes. I'm kind of set in my ways and don't take directions from producers very well, but I knew this case was important so I toned down my attitude.

I was taken to the place that Jackie was last seen and I "knew" that she had left willingly, so we moved on to the suspect's house. As I stood in front of his house, I tried to focus on the most valuable information that I could give the family. I'm pretty good at knowing the time the missing in question will be found, and providing a time line for the family is an immeasurable comfort for obvious reasons. When the missing person is alive, it tells the family when they will get their loved one back, and if the missing is deceased, it lets the family know the same thing with the additional comfort of knowing they will be able to lay their loved one to rest.

The producer asked me, "When will Jackie be found?"

I quickly shot back, "within two weeks." I could literally see the words "TWO WEEKS" as plain as day in front of me, as if I were reading a road sign. I continued with my other information, including that I was "seeing" Jackie's funeral. It was important for the family to know that they'd be able to have a memorial for her and be given a proper time to mourn. I was able to give the family lots of information on the perpetrator, such as motive for the crime, but in my heart I knew this was less important to them.

On Sunday, February 18, 2007, Jackie Hartman's remains were found thirteen and a half days after I had made my prediction. I cannot tell you how it feels to "know" when remains will be recovered and then hear on the news that your time frame was right. I was proud of myself and so relieved that the Hartmans now knew where their daughter was. Some may not understand this, but anyone who's had a missing loved one will understand.

When I was in my "zone" seeing through the killer's eyes, which I do by closing my eyes and concentrating on connecting to the perpetrator, I was able to see the two-lane road that I described her being close to as well as a dirt hill and see Jackie rolled down the mound of dirt. I had been able to get a strong impression of a "city limits" sign, which told me that she was outside the city she lived in, and this was confirmed later with the discovery of her body. There also aren't many two-lane roads, so Joe and I had figured out that she was off Route 87. She was in fact found off 87, but not in the area that we expected; he took Jackie in the opposite direction.

I think it is important for people to understand why reading a vision can be tricky. My cameraman and Joe, who know streets better than I do, assumed that she would be off 87 closest to her house, but she was in fact north of her home. This is why it's important for a medium/psychic always to work from his or her information alone, because once other people try to apply your information it can become tainted with their own ideas. Now, keep in mind that they were just trying to help find her, and their help was appreciated. It's just an example for learning purposes of why my information has to be passed directly to the family or the law just as I had said it word for word without my family or friends' input. I say this for intuitive people who ask the advice of their friends about a prediction, and then the prediction becomes a little muddled. Stick with your exact words and work through it solo to preserve the purity of your information.

It is interesting that with directions such as north, south, east, and west I tend to get turned around when driving, and the same can occur when I'm having a vision and I'm looking down a road and I'm not sure in which direction the assailant is fleeing. So I try and steer clear of north, south, east, and west and stick to road signs and describing the surroundings.

I had told the producers that I did not "see" that Jackie was killed at the suspect's house, and we confirmed this through details that surfaced later that supported my intuition that will be released at the appropriate time. I also sensed that Jackie could hear the traffic going by her as well as helicopters flying over where her body was left, and now I know this for sure because one of my friends in law enforcement told me later on that he had flown right over where Jackie's body was in his friend's helicopter. Her body was found a short distance off a two-lane highway and helicopters were combing the area where she had been left by the perpetrator. There is a suspect in custody who is awaiting trial for murder, so out of respect for the family, and the ongoing legal prosecution, the rest of my information will remain private.

My working Jackie's case was important for Jackie's family, but it impacted my life as well. I had an epiphany: I realized that it was time for me to hang up my hat and not work cases anymore. Every case takes a toll on me, and I was emotionally depleted. Even though I was satisfied with the job I had done, after seven years of working cases I felt like I was spinning my wheels. I felt like there would never be an end to working cases, and it wasn't my passion. It doesn't fill a void in me like so many people feel when they are on the right path. Instead, working cases has created a void in me, that never seems to be filled.

I have to practice what I preach, and when you reach a point in life where you need a change, you have to go with that feeling. So I want to thank everyone for their support and let all of the families of the victims whose cases I've worked on know that their loved ones will always be a part of me and the life I live.

Lights, Cameras, Action!

The second life-changing reading was orchestrated by a television show as well, and it involved two people I had never met before whom I was there to "read." The only information the show provided was the first names of the "sitters" (the living people for whom I'm bringing the deceased through). I sat in my hotel room with paper and a pen, writing down the impressions I was getting connected to Mary and Wade, the sitters.

The reading was taped for a television show, and we had never met prior to the reading. My first impression of Mary was the tidal wave of pain that I felt was walled up inside of her. I could also feel what a good person she was, with a kind heart. This is important, because it's essential for a medium to feel connected to the sitter. I then shook Wade's hand. He was somewhat skeptical, but I still felt connected to him. When a person looks at a reading with healthy skepticism, he is still completely readable.

We started out with my explaining my process—

what steps I take during a reading. I told them that I write before I meet the people whom I read and start off by reading my information.

I asked Mary if she had a daughter. She replied, "Yes, I have three daughters."

I continued with, "Is your daughter passed?"

She responded, "Yes."

That meant that I had made the connection with the daughter right off the bat, which made me happy. I went on to tell Mary that I felt a lot of pain in my head and that her daughter would have felt this at her time of passing due to head trauma. Her daughter Candace also said that she didn't take responsibility for her own passing and that it was entirely someone else's fault that she passed when she did. She went on to show herself leaning against a car, which told me that a vehicle had something to do with her passing.

I told them, "Your daughter said that she was bounced out of her body," and asked if that made sense to them.

Mary and Wade whispered, "Yes."

It turned out that Candace was hit by a car driven by a woman who, authorities say, was drugged up on prescription medication but had chosen to risk driving anyway. Who died and how is always core in a reading, and often the deceased comes through with this information first as a way to identify himself or herself. There were many pieces of information that I enjoyed receiving. Yes, I said enjoyed! When I conduct a reading, I don't just feel the hard stuff. I also get to feel the love and humor that the deceased loved one still has. Candace has a fantastic sense of humor as well as a lot of love for Mary and Wade, which made the reading quite wonderful for me.

Mary asked me to inquire about Candace's brother, Jake, to see if Candace had a message for him. I told her that earlier I had gotten the name Jack connected to Candace. Mary was happy to hear this since Jack is Candace's father, who was not present at the reading. After this had been established, I gave her the information she had requested on Jake.

Candace also came through with the name Christopher, and she showed it to me over and over until I shared it with Wade, who told me that his middle name is Christopher. Since I already knew that Wade was her husband's first name, it makes sense to me that she gave me his middle name, a part of him that I couldn't know, to let him know that she acknowledges him by name.

Candace kept saying, "Happy birthday!" and she kept showing me birthday balloons. I passed this on to Mary and Wade, who looked somewhat perplexed. I explained that she was saying it for a close family member and that the birthday was not in February but rather January. Since we were just inside February, I felt it was important to specify that I was clearly seeing "JANUARY" written out in front of my eyes. They still couldn't put their finger on it, and I blurted out, "Her father-in-law, your dad, Wade, did his birthday just pass?" Well, we were finally on the same page. Wade acknowledged that his dad's birthday was at the end of January and it had occurred a couple of weeks prior to our reading.

I think this example of how I had to keep going back to Candace for more information demonstrates the interaction between mediums and the deceased. I couldn't have been reading Mary and Wade's minds, because they weren't remembering the information that Candace had given me. As far as they knew consciously, there were no recent birthdays in the family. Readings can be emotionally draining for the people receiving a reading, and they need the medium and the deceased to be as specific as possible or they miss out on some of the great messages.

An interesting thing happened during this reading that is an absolute rarity. This can happen, it just doesn't come around very often. While I was bringing through Candace, a deceased teenage girl whom I had brought through years before for her own mom started coming through too. I was very confused by this, but I thought that maybe because they both had died in vehicle accidents at a young age, the teenage girl felt connected to Candace.

Mind you, while this was all going on I had cameras on every angle of my face, and I was under a little bit of pressure to do a solid reading for Mary and Wade plus a good TV show. So I was juggling the charades from the teenager, paying attention to Candace's messages, and also staying focused on Mary and Wade's well-being, making sure that my messages were delivered with compassion and precision.

My attention was pulled by the teenager as she began showing me things that had come through in her reading for her mother, like the Chinese restaurant, the car, and loving her mom. They all were being thrown at me in a flurry, and I started getting overwhelmed. Then the teenage girl whom I hadn't seen in years stood before me and pointed to my book *We Are Their Heaven* that I had previously signed for Mary and was leaning against the foot of her chair.

All of a sudden I said, "Mary, can I see your book?" I picked up her book as though I had tunnel vision. I realized that in my previous book in the loss of child chapter, I had written about the teenage girl who was now coming through and I had given her a different name to hide her identity. I had called her Candace, Mary's daughter's real name. They both had died too young due to head trauma and internal injuries from vehicle accidents, and the teenage girl had been trying to get me to say "Candace." Aarrgghhh! I didn't put it together until after Mary had shared her daughter's name with me. Then it immediately clicked in my head what the charades were intended to convey.

I turned to the page with Candace's name on it and showed it to Mary. That completely floored her, but at the same time it was hauntingly special. In addition to the huge impact behind the meaning of the name Candace in Mary's reading, I believe the reading was a way for the teenager again to reach her parents through me as a sort of a sign that she's very much still around. So I knew that it was very important for me to publish this part of the reading.

I loved knowing that Candace and one of my favorite teenagers had met on the otherside, and I shared this with Mary, who was impressed that the spelling of Candace's name was correct. Why I named the sweet teenager Candace is hard to say; I don't know anyone named Candace. I think the name was given to me through divine intervention. Well before Candace's life was cut short I was writing her name in my previous book and now again in *Secrets of the Monarch* after her death. I am honored to know both families connected to the two young ladies who have now touched us all through their grace and humor.

Candace was a wonderful example of a daughter/wife/mother who knew she was loved by her family and spent her time wisely while alive by connecting with people, showing affection to those she loved, and living life without regret. Since Candace had died much too young, she will spend time around her husband and young son as well as her entire family until she decides otherwise, and that's the beauty of "those who live again"—they have the power to be wherever their heaven resides. We spend our days being so hard on ourselves for every little thing in life that often we don't recognize that we are someone else's idea of heaven.

Prior to the first reading I had written "daughter" on a piece of paper and I was able to hand this to Mary before we got started. Gestures like that can make a reading very powerful. I was aware that I hadn't written as much as I normally do in the notes that I take as the deceased dictate them to me, so this told me that the good stuff would come out during our follow-up meeting back in Arizona. When I had first met Mary, I had commented that her daughter had gone to a lot of trouble arranging to bring me to Mary and Candace's husband, Wade. Mary laughed because she knew that it was true. I felt a great connection with Mary and Wade, and I knew that it wasn't the last time that I would see them.

Monday, February 19, Mary arrived at my house for a reading because I felt there were things that Candace hadn't said in front of the cameras for the show because it was a little too impersonal. The second wave of this reading was to let Mary know that Candace was there for her whenever her mom needed her, not just the day of filming but always. When Mary showed up, we hugged and she said, "How are you?"

I said, "Honestly I'm a little frazzled. A few moments ago I found out that Jackie Hartman's body was just recovered." I felt a connection to both of their families, and both young ladies seemed to be very good at moving mountains for their family's peace of mind. I thought it was very profound that two weeks after the show I would reconnect to both of the deceased. Jackie was reconnected to me through the press and the news of finding her body, which caused me to feel for her family on the highest level. Candace would reconnect to me through my follow-up reading with Mary. That day I felt them both around me, but I needed to clear my head and focus on Candace because Mary was in front of me and I was eager to see what messages Candace had for her family.

I had held back a piece of information in the first reading that involved Wade, Candace's husband, which is very rare for me to do. Candace had played the song "How to Save a Life" by the Fray over and over again in my head, but I didn't see how the lyrics would apply to Wade or how it could make him feel better. I always have to weigh the potential of hurting someone I "read" against delivering the entire message from the deceased. I can't injure the living to speak for the dead. Anyway, it's a beautiful song, but I had never before had anyone come through with it, so this was a unique situation. I shared my dilemma with Mary, and then I heard Candace whisper "organ donor" in my ear, so I asked Mary, "Did Candace donate organs that saved people's lives?"

Mary said, "Yes. She donated three organs, saved three people's lives."

Then it clicked in my head. Candace wanted Wade to know that "How to Save a Life" was the song that would let him know that she was around him and also let him know that she lives on in many ways.

I told Mary, "Wade was probably pretty conflicted over having to deal with the topic of organ donation at a time when he was losing his wife, so it makes perfect sense that Candace would be letting Wade know that she's still intact and happy that she was able to help people in need."

Candace shared with her mom that she was around "Jack." She had mentioned him by name in our first reading and now she was mentioning him again. I knew from Mary's confirmation in the first reading that Jack is Candace's father.

"Mary, Candace says to tell you that there is another Jack and to let you know that she's around him. His name was John but they called him Jack."

Mary explained that, Candace's dad and grand-dad were John and they are both called Jack.

Candace was letting her family know that she was with her grandfather, which is very comforting for families. To be able to grasp that older generations can spend time with the younger ones and take care of them on the otherside is a wonderful gift from the past generations, and it says a lot about the living who are able to understand the concept of eternal connections.

Another piece of information that I loved was when Candace spoke of planting trees and flowers as a memorial to her. She was showing gratitude to the people who loved her enough to memorialize her. Mary confirmed that two memorials were being put together for Candace and both involved planting trees and flowers at the schools where Candace and Mary taught. When a person dies, he or she observes the butterfly effect that the death set in motion and often mention this sort of detail in readings. When Mary was leaving, I told her that Candace was telling me that "she was going to send her mom flowers over the next few months through different people."

Candace told me to turn around, and as I turned I saw the roses in a vase on my kitchen counter. She told me to take one out. I did as Candace said and handed it to Mary.

"Mary, this is the first rose to come to you from Candace through living people connected to her. It's a way for her to send you her love when you need it the most."

Two days later Mary emailed me to tell me that a student she had when he was in the third grade and who was now a senior in high school had brought her a dozen roses for no reason. Mary said she was shocked because she hadn't seen her former student in years. Mary knew that the roses were from Candace, that Candace had orchestrated the gift. Mary remembered my words—or should I say Candace's words—from the reading and was touched on a very personal level. Mary has received others since.

When I write a book, it's personally important to me to show both sides of a reading, because the medium and the sitter are separate factors in a reading. Each comes away with pieces of information that mean something different to everyone involved. In order to give a fuller picture of the reading, I have included Mary's take in her own words as well as her advice to others who have suffered a similar loss to her own. I believe that no one can fully understand what it's like to suffer a specific type of loss, such as the loss of a child, unless he or she has been through it personally, and Mary's intention in sharing her story of loss is to help others who have walked the same sort of path that she has walked.

You will notice that the information that meant the most to her is emotionally based and centered around the nuances that were her daughter. My take on the reading focused on the specifics, such as the names, physical descriptions, vacation spots, etc., because as a medium it's crucial that I deliver the concrete details connected to the deceased and the living and then fill that in with the emotional words of comfort provided by the deceased. Without the concrete details, sitters couldn't, for obvious reasons, let down their emotional guard to receive the words of comfort.

It is a rare occurrence for my readers to see both the medium's side as well as the sitter's because readings are so personal. I know that showing the bigger picture will help people to understand what a reading entails as well as how a reading has the potential to reinforce that those who go before us still have the capacity to remain with us and hear us. Now that you've heard my take on the reading, you can have insight into Mary's experience both with the loss of her daughter as well as her reading with me. It's very personal for Mary to allow the world a glimpse into her tragedy, so I thank her for her selflessness in helping others to understand what she's been through and how she perseveres.

In Mary's Words

How does a mother describe the pain and loss of losing a child? It is indescribable. The pain is deep-rooted within who you are, whom you love, whom you nurtured and protected for many years. The dreams you had for your child disappear with her death, and a life with such a purpose suddenly vanishes from sight. The pain is brutal. It's as if this stranger who killed your child ripped a piece of your heart out of your body . . . and you know it will never be replaced. The heartache doesn't leave you for one minute, even when you appear to be doing something else. The veil of sadness and despair that you wear becomes a part of your everyday wardrobe. You can't run from the pain, and words you never thought you'd hear connected to your child, like "deceased," "dead," and "gone," are now rolling off the lips of everyone who knows about your loss. These feelings and experiences are all unfortunately a normal part of grieving the loss of your child.

I know with all my heart that Candace orchestrated the reading with Allison. I know that Candace sent us to Allison. Her presence and spirit, I believe, have guided me since her death, and this was confirmed through the reading with Allison. As I tearfully wrote the story of her life and death for the show's producers, I felt Candace was guiding my fingers as her story started to unfold upon the computer screen. I had just opened my heart to some stranger on a computer who I knew probably wouldn't even read my words, and they were some of the most important words that I would ever communicate. I no sooner pushed the "send" icon when I received a phone call asking if our family would be willing to come cross-country for a reading. Within a few days, my son-in-law Wade and I were sitting down with Allison. Wade and I both knew it was Candace's doing. For both of us to travel across the country in a matter of days was no coincidence. My daughter had a "get it done now" attitude and a heart filled with compassion, and her purpose was to communicate with her family, son, Wade, and myself.

I never thought a parent's worst nightmare would come true for me, but it did the evening of August 23, 2006. My beautiful, spirited thirty-one-year-old daughter, mother, wife, and sister, Candace, was run over while riding her bike toward the sunset on a warm summer's eve. How could this have happened? She had a fourteen-month-old son who fulfilled her in every way. She had an amazing husband who was devoted to her. She had a mother, father, sisters, and a brother who loved her. She had a classroom full of students waiting for her to teach them. She had plans and she had worked so hard to get to where she was in life. The information that I needed to know the most was, did she feel the pain? Did she hear us at the hospital? What does she want us to do now? These questions and many more were answered as Allison communicated Candace's thoughts, memories, and humor during our reading.

Within minutes of the reading, I knew Allison was authentic. I was touched by her warmth and sincerity. That was essential for us from the onset of our journey. We were there for Candace, and I soon realized that Allison was there for us. As soon as Allison began to speak, I felt Candace's presence. Allison's tone and twinkle in her eye reminded me of Candace. One of the first things Allison said to Wade and me was that she saw "distance" between the two of us, meaning that we weren't physically close by. Wade lives in California and I live in Arizona. "Okay," I thought, "she is on to something." Then Allison turned to me and said, "The deceased one calls herself your shadow." That was the point where I knew Candace was speaking through Allison. You see, Candace and I would speak of that quite often, you know, the good characteristics as well as the not so good ones she inherited. Allison would not know that Candace and I have very similar personalities, are highly emotional, both chose teaching as a profession, and we both have similar physical characteristics. That doesn't apply to all mothers and daughters.

Allison's messages were heartfelt and even brought her to subtle tears at times as she reassured me that "she's already heard everything you have to say before you ever met me. You know." Other messages showed Candace's laughter and spunk as she told Wade that "she still sleeps on her side on the bed so stay off of it." Allison described a picture of Wade and Candace in Hawaii beside a palm tree on the beach that Wade had only recently found. Coincidence? I think not. Candace reminded Wade to keep the vision of the way she looked on her wedding day in his mind, a vision I know he will never forget. During the reading, Candace spoke about her father, sisters, and brother with details about their personalities and relationship that only Candace would know. She told her brother Jake that she was "proud" of him. Candace had spoken those words many times before. Allison described how Candace wanted her sisters each to have a piece of her jewelry, and Candace passed a message to me to give to her sister Amy, telling her to "slow down." This made perfect sense to me! Candace spoke of how much she loved my mother and that she continues to be around her and that my mom would smile even when things were bad. Yes! That is my mother, Candace's grandma!

Allison described Candace as a young girl to a T. Her hair pulled two sides up, blond curls hanging down her back, and in a dress. Every picture that I own of Candace as a young girl is that vision. In fact, after Candace's death, a very good friend of mine bought me a painting of a young girl just like the many pictures that I have of Candace. It hangs in our family room as a memorial of Candace, so to speak, not that we will ever forget her.

Losing a daughter in such a brutal way is horrific in itself, but every time I look into my young grandson's eyes I see a child who will never know the gentle mother who loved every minute of her life with him. A mother who read books, organized playgroups for him, and took him to many different places so that he could experience all life has to offer. I will never forget the words spoken through Allison regarding Candace's son, reassuring Wade and me that she has not left him because "she says she's his angel and always will be." Allison went on to tell us that Candace sits at the end of his bed and that she will come to him in his dreams. Wade says that Owen randomly says "Mommy," as though he knows she's there still. If you knew my daughter, you would absolutely know that she would never leave her son, even after her death.

Our family had recently talked about how we wanted to celebrate Candace's upcoming birthday. We thought about having a celebration of her life by sending off balloons and having her son help to make a cake. Allison told us that Candace said, "Thank you for celebrating my birthday." And Allison indicated that Candace meant after her death. She heard us plan this! We are so happy to know that she will be there with us!

Allison's gift showered Wade and me with Candace's undying love. Candace loves Wade with all her heart, and that was conveyed through Allison loud and clear. Candace said that "Wade made her so happy and she was eternally grateful for the wonderful life that he gave to her so lovingly."

Through Allison, Candace reassured us that her gentle spirit continues to guide her son, and knowing that he will be like her and that he will "know" her filled our hearts with hope. Allison described too many details that only Candace's immediate family, Wade or I, would know. Allison reassured Candace's dad, sisters, and brother that Candace's love will continue and she will always be with us, just not in the normal physical way that she was before. Wade and I were overwhelmed by the amount of details that Allison conveyed. Candace told us repeatedly that she loved us and that she was grateful for such a wonderful family. Candace said she knows that our family will be there for her son and Wade and that she really appreciates that.

Candace had said that the accident wasn't her fault and that she had no hand in it. We knew that. The pain? Candace said there wasn't any more pain for her and that her spirit was bounced out immediately. Thank God for that. And she heard us at the hospital . . . loving her, touching her, and holding her one last time. For this information, we will be forever grateful to Allison.

Mediums? Never really gave them much thought. I really didn't need to think of mediums. I believe in life after death, so why should I care about mediums? I believe that heaven is glorious and that all those who lead a good life will reach their destiny. Skeptical? Probably. I must admit, Allison DuBois has changed my life and has given Wade and me the tools, belief, and knowledge to talk to Candace whenever we want to, and believe me, I do.

You see, my daughter Candace was a powerful and intelligent woman, and I knew that she was not finished with us. I thank Candace every day for arranging the reading with Allison. She knew that only through someone like Allison, someone of the highest caliber, would Wade and I really believe and know for sure that she was not gone. The Lord sent us a gift to help us through all of our pain and grief. The gift was Allison. A sincere, authentic, and dedicated woman or, as we say, "the real deal."

Do I cry? Daily. Am I still grieving? Oh, yes. The pain is engulfing and it can consume you. I think of my daughter every minute of every day. I wish I could turn the clock back. Do I talk about our reading to everyone we know? No. A reading is a very personal, loving "discussion" with your deceased loved one. Some people need to be at a reading to believe; others already believe. I know Candace believes, because the force of her voice, spirit, and energy rang out loud and clear that evening through Allison and continues to be with us when we need Candace the most.

Losing someone you love so much is painful, especially someone young, full of positive energy and purpose in life. I can speak only as a mother that the road that I have had to walk down these past six months is one that I wish upon no one. So in my writing, I hope that I can provide a small calmness or peace to those who have lost a loved one by letting you know that our kids remain with us even after death, as do the rest of our loved ones. If you listen really closely and you talk to that special person, she will let you know that she is with you one way or another. It may not be in the way you expect, but she is there, guiding you. I will be forever thankful that

Allison could gently take me by the hand and guide me to feel the spirit of my daughter Candace that will sustain me for now, until Candace and I meet again.

A couple of weeks later, when I did the follow-up reading, Mary told me that I have the same light in my eyes that Candace had. It is one of the most meaningful compliments anyone has ever given me. It was amusing that when Mary and I would start up a conversation about a current topic, Candace would want to weigh in with her opinion and I would pass her words on to Mary, who would then laugh that the words that I used were exactly what her daughter would have said (as I reminded Mary, Candace *did* say them).

I told Mary that I know Candace pulled a lot of strings to make the first reading happen, and I felt compelled to help Mary past the one-year anniversary of Candace's death. At the time of Mary's reading, it had been less than six months since her daughter was killed by a driver who, authorities claim, was drugged up on prescription medication and had run over a fire hydrant and a parking meter right before hitting Candace with her car, so Candace's family was still quite emotionally raw.

We await the trial of the driver, but, regardless of its outcome, here's a message to my readers: if you are impaired by drugs or alcohol—and this goes for prescription drugs as well, like the driver had consumed before the fateful night that Candace was hit—don't get behind the wheel! It takes only one time to kill someone and change a family forever. I don't see any difference between a person shooting a gun in the air knowing he could kill someone when the bullet comes down and getting behind the wheel of a car under the influence of drugs or alcohol. If you see someone swerving, call the police and get him off the road. Calling a cab is a small price to pay to save a life. Consider Candace, a very special spokesperson from the otherside whose death was tragically unnecessary. Let's not allow Candace to have died in vain. Someone can save a life, and you never know when the life saved will be your own. I'm always asked about worthwhile charities for people to donate their time or money to, and I support MADD, Mothers Against Drunk Driving. They have helped to save many lives through education, and I know that Candace instigated my writing this in my book, so there you go.

My mom had recently moved a great distance away, and I really felt comforted to know Mary, who is very maternal and has a lot to teach. I hope that I too can help teach her how to reconnect with Candace in a very strong way so that one day she will communicate with her daughter directly and not through a glorified secretary to the dead like me. Candace was fascinating to me because, like some deceased I've brought through before, she sees herself as "alive" with some limitations, as she knows it's our energy inside that truly makes us "alive." I've met physically living people who were "dead" inside. Which is more effective in emotionally touching others? That's something everyone should think about.

As Mary and I parted ways that day, I assured her that I was going to help her through this, although it is rare for me to befriend someone I read. I got around this rule by deciding Mary was technically not a client because I hadn't charged her for my services. At the end of our meeting, I came to my second epiphany for the day: I missed reading people, connecting to them personally, and it resonated within me that it was time to go back to private readings. I had always loved doing them. Working cases, something I did from time to time, had truly taken over my life. I no longer felt that I could do it anymore.

Maybe one day I'll go back to occasional cases, but for now I just want to do what I love and connect with the living through the deceased and vice versa. I want to feel the love that they still have for each other and see what made the deceased happy during their lives. I miss the smiles that appeared on the faces of the people I read despite their tears flowing.

I love when I get a spirit with a sense of humor who cracks a joke that makes the living loved one laugh just like old times. The deceased show me photographs of their weddings, babies, holidays, vacations, etc., and they tell me about the good old days; they show me their life through their eyes. I can smell the cakes they baked or the cigars they smoked, although usually not from the same person! They share with me a potpourri of memories that constructed their life, and their memories tell me a story of those that they touched. So I'm sure that anyone can understand why I miss experiences like that. It's easy to get wrapped up in the tapestry of other people's lives, and I want to learn what they have to teach.

Here's something for science-minded people to think about. Sir Isaac Newton derived the first law of thermodynamics; energy cannot be created or destroyed; it can only be changed from one form to another.

If the energy that we are made of cannot be destroyed, then where does it go? And doesn't it make a lot of sense that the souls I communicate with are energy that has simply been changed from one form to another after shedding the body, and they are still able to communicate, only in a different way now because they have to learn how to access the living by connecting to our own energy? I believe that mediums feel vibrations that turn into forms of communication from the deceased. A good metaphor is that canines can hear a whistle that humans can't. Is it possible that some humans can also hear on a unique level, or is it possible that a medium's energy is being manipulated by the deceased so that their communication seems to us to be audible? Maybe we think that we see the deceased standing before us because he or she has accessed parts of our brain that once a pattern of pieces are put together gives us a full image of a person.

The deceased also must learn how to speak to us without using their voice as they did in life, so is it possible that they access a medium's experiences through her brain waves to try to convey messages through images flashed in her mind, in front of her very eyes, through frequencies of sound or her nervous system? Like a great opera singer can match the frequency of a crystal wineglass with his voice, and if the pitch is held long enough with a steady common frequency, the glass will break. It would make sense that the frequency of the energy of our soul that is left behind after the death of our body could be matched by the living's energy and make it possible to communicate with them through a common vibration to their own, and this includes their being able to manipulate people and objects. Newton said that energy could not be destroyed and that energy could change from one form to another, therefore if energy has the capacity to change to another form, then it's possible that the energy could have the ability to adapt to other energies and interact.

When I do a reading, it seems to me that my own memories can be accessed by the deceased by their adjusting to my energy frequency, and after that they can access the words they need to communicate with me through hitting the right frequency to trigger a "feeling" in me. For instance, I know what "Hawaii" feels like to me. I've been there, I know what the air smells like and what the vibe of the state is. Once the deceased triggers the feeling in me that is "Hawaii," that translates through my system, and as a medium I see the word "Hawaii" in my head and so the deceased has successfully communicated through me. I know what piano music feels like. I can identify a piano, and so the deceased would use what I know about the subject to get me to say, "I'm seeing a piano connected to the deceased, so that tells me he played the piano." Sometimes this is communicated to me through my thinking that I hear a piano note being played in my ear, so what I hear as a sound from a piano in reality may not be audible but rather a frequency that translates as "piano" in my mind. If a spirit wants me to say "father," he or she pulls an emotional lever that triggers my dad's energy, which then allows me to know that the deceased is the sitter's father. I'm still getting used to "sister" energy since I don't have any sisters, and identifying a sister coming through can be harder for me. I think you get the idea of what I'm saying.

The deceased who lived very full lives and connected with people are better at connecting with a medium because their energy knew how to empathize with others in life. Empathy energetically is the ability to stand in another's shoes, so the deceased would seem to have an easier time adjusting energetically to my frequency, getting a sense of me, and in turn accessing me as a medium.

It also seems to me that the deceased who were very emotional and felt a lot for others come through more easily in readings than those who were dry or emotionless. I can effortlessly pull impressions off the deceased who laughed a lot in life; they had personalities that raised other's spirits energetically. I think it's likely that people who experienced a lot of great emotions in life have the ability to function at a higher frequency that sustains their soul after their body is gone, and they maintain a similar frequency to the living.

Those who didn't do much in life and were energy suckers didn't have a lot of motivating energy that fueled others, so in death, minus their body they don't have a strong enough soul to function on a similar frequency to the living. In life, their body allowed them to communicate with others through talking, sex, writing, and many different ways, so without their body their energy isn't able to connect with the living on its own.

We've all met people who have endless energy and we all want to know where they get it so that we can go get some too. They have a tendency to lift people up and energetically prod others to be more like them, which is good. It's part of why we love actors and singers so much—they "project" their energy to us and we can emotionally "feed" off their energy by drawing it in. When I conduct a reading and the deceased has a bit of a weak personality, I have to pull extra energy off the living person I'm reading and concentrate harder to make sense of what the deceased is trying to say because his or her energy is faint to me.

I know that one day there will be a greater understanding of why a medium is able to act as a conduit between the living and dead. I further believe we will even be able to identify a genetic marker that runs in families of people with various abilities. Even though we don't have all the answers surrounding the spirits or those of us who can communicate with them, that doesn't mean they don't exist. Human DNA has existed for as long as human beings have been here, and in the 1980s science began to understand the significance of it and identify it. But just because there wasn't a scientific stamp of approval on DNA long ago didn't mean it didn't exist. It just wasn't understood yet.

I see mediums and the afterlife in very much the same light as many other parts of life that have been persecuted or misunderstood in the past. There is no one to blame. It's just a matter of us learning, keeping an open mind, and evolving just as we've done in the past.

I hope that my being able to share with you what I've learned from our deceased loved ones has gotten your wheels turning about what you know and what you believe. I know that my husband's wheels are turning so fast there's smoke coming out of his ears. He loves any opportunity to try to apply science to what I do by documenting my predictions and logging when they come to pass. I personally like making world predictions and Joe loves writing them down and watching them come to fruition. It's something we do together. I'll provide you with some examples of predictions that I've made over the last few years so that you get the idea of how my visions work.

On July 8, 2001, I had a vision of an astronaut in a spacecraft that exploded. I asked Joe, "Has only one space shuttle exploded?"

Joe replied, "Yes, one shuttle and also one Apollo test run."

"Joe, he shows me another space shuttle exploding other than those two explosions. He illustrates it as being 'like the *Challenger.*' "

I went on to describe the man who was conveying this message to me. I saw him in a white space suit with a metal collar and an American flag patch on his arm with a bubble helmet. He was in his forties. I described a wire causing the explosion. My brilliant husband later identified him as Gus Grissom, who had died in the *Apollo 1* test run on January 27, 1967, when his capsule caught fire on the launch pad. In my vision, I saw this man in an explosion "of yellow like the rising sun looks in orbit."

As I interacted with Gus, I sensed that he was a humble man. I described him as a hero, yet he said he "felt more like a pioneer." I still say that he's a hero. He showed me Saturn's rings and Jupiter, and said, "There's going to be a shift in the spin that is going to shift how the light falls and will allow life to grow. Jupiter and Saturn should be watched closely, and they are not, not necessarily the moons."

Although the planets and space were important to him, his most important message dealt with his "family." Normally I don't comment on people I don't know, but somehow I have to convey this message. It is not harmful in any way, and I'm not even sure that it will get to them, but I'm doing it because he asked me to. Gus said, "I want my family to know that they were the last thing that ran through my mind before I died."

On February 1, 2003, the Space Shuttle *Columbia* exploded in space. A year and a half had passed since an astronaut named Gus told me that this day was coming. You can understand my dilemma. I couldn't call NASA and share my vision; they would have laughed their ass off. I intervene only when I'm put in a position to help, and here I didn't feel that I was. I'm sure that Gus took care of the *Columbia* crew as if they were his own, and I know that our country appreciates their bravery.

On April 24, 2002, I made the prediction that a huge archaeological find would reveal what scientists would believe to be an Egyptian queen's tomb. Two weeks later, on May 9, it was reported that archaeologists had uncovered what they believed to be an Egyptian queen's tomb.

On November 29, 2004 I had a vision that the pope would die in 2005 and Joe detailed the prediction in his journal. The pope passed away on April 2, 2005. I saw the person who would replace the pope as more current and changing rules laid down by the church long ago.

That same day I also made a prediction that George W. Bush would survive an assassination attempt. On May 10, 2005, an assassination attempt was made on his life.

I've shared with you only a few of the many predictions that I've made concerning future events around the world. Some I won't reveal because tempers can flare when it's a political prediction. Unfortunately, some of the predictions involve tragedy, but many bring great hope for the world. In 2005, I saw medical strides being made and that organs would be able to be grown outside the body. This has happened and it's very exciting. Cancer will be cured, and the fact that I'll be here to see it is thrilling to me. Although there are life-changing events still to take place, you have to look to the future with great expectations and faith.

CHAPTER 10

The Real Allison DuBois

*M*any of you have gotten to know a little of my story through the hit TV show *Medium*. I am lucky enough to be brilliantly portrayed by Patricia Arquette, and Joe is portrayed by the excellent Jake Weber, who is completely freaked out by me. The only thing we have in common is we both have a pug dog. That's a good thing to have in common. Jake's a really great guy, and as all my fans point out, he's easy on the eyes. All the actors portraying my friends and family are very dear to our hearts, as you can imagine. Part of the reason I write my books is to share with you the real story of my life so that you have the wonderful dramatic version of my life on

Medium and the comparably dramatic life that I know as mine that all began in Phoenix years ago.

I try to end each book by updating you on the highs and lows of my life since my last book, so here's what I have learned this year. I'll start with some of the low points so that I can end on a positive note.

After becoming a public figure, I learned that journalists don't always print the truth about you, as many of my celebrity friends had warned me would happen, and you'll never get an apology for the reporter's lack of truth. There was a journalist—I use that term loosely—who wrote a story about me that was completely erroneous and that attacked my character. I can't even begin to convey the confusion that plagues me when people make up things about me to suit their argument, and this goes not only for reporters but also people who used to be in my life who try to hold on to me even if it's just by bad-mouthing me. It's weird. The magazines don't apologize for being misleading and the reporters want to stay as far away from the angry subject of their story as possible.

The reporter didn't do his homework and I believe intentionally ignored the information that supported me. What happened to unbiased reporting? He seemed to have missed the truth that *Paula Zahn Now* on CNN found through good investigative reporting, which was that the local sheriff's office confirmed

that it met with me about a case and that the Texas
Rangers put me in touch with them.

There had been a question around my first case of
whether or not I actually had worked with the Texas
Rangers years ago, and it is a fact that I did work with
them. Due to what I believe to be politics within
the Rangers organization, they won't admit having
worked with me, but outside organizations have confirmed my connection in the media, since they were
present when I was picked up from the airport by the
Rangers. I've never charged for a case or expenses, so
I don't get the resistance. I find that those who asked
for my help in the first place come down with amne-
sia when questioned about their association with me,
but I always say, you don't break a glass ceiling without getting cut.

I'll never understand what people are so afraid of,
but I know the truth and you have to believe in yourself. If you let people break your spirit and detour
you from your path, then you have not been true to
yourself or those you're here to touch, those who believe in you. I recently realized that sometimes it's
hard to take my own advice, which my husband and
friends repeat back to me verbatim. They say that
they once heard it from a wise woman, which makes
me laugh.

In everyone's life there comes a time when somebody will take a shot at your character. I let it affect me for a day and then I remember that I tell people to write down what makes them mad and burn the paper—it's therapeutic. But I decided that instead of burning it, I'd publish it. The best way to take the air out of the sails of those who try to take a shot at you is to expose them to the light. I've learned that people who sling mud at the wall to see what will stick are the same people who don't like the spotlight directed toward their own character. So see that? I energetically transferred my own frustration back onto those who have written untruths about me, and I restored balance within me once again.

Write down what troubles you in your life and then think about what you can do to turn a negative into a positive. For me, writing down how I felt allowed me to energetically and physically let go of the untruths that a bad reporter scribbled down and published. I think that everyone has had something untrue said about him or her. But really, people can hurt you with words only if you let them.

I decided not to let the bastards get me down! Well said, don't you think?

People saying something bad about you doesn't make it true. Sticks and stones, remember? Afterward, I had a moment where I looked upward toward the big puffy clouds in the sky on a cold January day and asked, "Is this it? Is this what I have to do for the rest of my life?" I heard that soft, guiding voice that I've trusted since I was small say, "They can't take from you what you've been given." I paused and grinned with an awareness that a person rarely has in his or her life—you know, a defining moment. Then I was told, "You have hell in your eyes, but you hold heaven in your heart."

At that moment I proudly owned the description of me, along with a reminder that I couldn't let someone take from me what was never his or hers to have or to judge. Spiritual people have limits too. We're not born to be doormats, but I think people lose sight of that fact sometimes.

I had no idea that septic skeptics, as I like to call them, have clubs that send "one of their own" out to our events to give mediums a hard time. In their skeptic clubs they teach their members to get as much media attention as possible, talk louder than everyone else, and wear a hat of some sort. These are some of the rules that came straight from one of their meetings in a ballroom—we too have people to infiltrate their amusing gatherings! It's kind of ironic, if you think about it. They're reinforcing our significance, and I thank them for that compliment.

Mediums try to help those in need, giving much of themselves for others' peace of mind. We put forth monumental effort and would have it no other way. I always wonder if "professional skeptics" will ever find a new hobby. I know the answer to that. Oh, well. Roll with it, right? It's not an easy path to walk, but it's mine and I walk it proudly.

There were some big lessons for me to learn this year, but as long as I can turn a negative into a positive I'll continue to grow stronger. Nobody walks a pain-free path, but sometimes it helps to hear someone else's plight so that we know that for all of us it's an important part of realizing our depth and our ability to persevere.

Friction causes people to tighten up their senses and focus on identifying what caused it and how to deal with it—whether to get rid of the friction, make it work for you, or figure out how to neutralize it. It's all part of learning how to master your life and really grab the bull by the horns and ride the ride.

I hope that you find my coping skills helpful in your own life and remember to breathe. I know it sounds simple, but many people get so tense that their breathing becomes a series of short shallow breaths instead of deep cleansing breaths that really do help to put you in a better state of mind.

Another hurdle that I had to overcome this year involved reading a well-known woman who shall remain nameless. I was asked by this news anchor for a reading, and I obliged because I hoped that it would help her. She would sit with me for five minutes and then run out to tape a segment, come back for five, and run out again. I was honestly ready to leave, because I'm not used to conducting readings like that and, frankly, it was rude. So after her wasting a good hour or so of my time while I waited for her, she says, "Well, you could have looked that information up on the internet."

Wow! Why did she ask me to read her, then? First of all, her statement was entirely offensive. Second, she wasn't even interviewing me. It was another anchor, and reading her wasn't for the cameras or money or anything, and how could I know that I was going to read her in the first place? Unless I'm psychic, and then that kills her argument, anyway. There was no payoff in wasting my time. So the lesson was learned: don't read public figures because they are all over the internet (just kidding!).

I have read many other celebrities who were very happy with their readings, maybe because they stayed seated and listened to the messages. I think it was a personality thing; sometimes you just don't click. By the way, she didn't even say thank you. Now, that I can't understand; my family taught me better than that. She did, however, complain about some other famous mediums who had read her, and after her real manners surfaced I had to feel for the other mediums. A mind-blowing reading is just not possible when your sitter gets up and leaves every five minutes and returns ten to fifteen minutes later over and over again. So if you set up a reading, be sure that you listen carefully to the medium's information and don't walk in with a chip on your shoulder or an agenda. You're not denying the medium; you're denying the deceased who's trying to reach you.

What a year! Do you love my medium dirt? Still rolling with the punches! I know that these occurrences just go with the territory of life, and I'm not unique in this way. Another side effect of being a medium that I've had to just accept is that my presence messes with electronic equipment. I've found it to be more of a nuisance since the nineties began when everything seemed to become electronic and computerized. I thought it would be fun to share one example of how I can interfere with electronic gadgets anywhere, anytime. I also thought you'd appreciate hearing it in the journalist's own words.

In my thirty years as a journalist, I've had plenty of strange experiences. Getting stuck on a Utah mountaintop with Jon Bon Jovi. Helping Shannen Doherty with her dog when it fell into her pool. Meeting Faye Dunaway. Still, for pure unexpected shock, I'd have to say my first interview with Allison DuBois might top them all.

Allison and I first spoke when I was working on a story about her TV alter ego, Patricia Arquette. I met her on the set of *Medium* and I didn't know re-

ally what to expect. Before we began, she asked if
I'd brought a backup tape recorder because sometimes when she's around, odd things happen, and
she suggested that I take notes as well. Not the usual
way to begin an interview, but I didn't really think
anything of it.

We talked for about half an hour and, when we
were done, I played a few seconds of the tape back
to make sure that it had recorded everything. Instead of Allison's voice, there was silence. I rewound
a little more. Still silence. I went all the way back to
the start of the interview. Absolutely nothing there.
I had no idea how that could have happened, so to
test my recorder, I went into another room and
spoke into it. When I played that back, it was all
perfectly clear. I did other interviews the rest of that
day. There was no problem with the recorder.

It's easy to be cynical about Allison, but if my
experience with her taught me anything, it's to keep
an open mind about everything. And write her
quotes down by hand next time instead of electron-
ically recording them.—Craig Tomashoff

Last year also held some wonderful moments that
serve as the peaks rather than the valleys I just shared
with you. I toured the U.K. for my second book,
which was greatly entertaining. I yelled over the pal-
ace gate that I was related to the queen, but they

didn't buy it. Oh, well. While I was in London I met some great people. At the Sci Fi Channel especially, Niki, my publicist, made me feel welcome for the kickoff of *Medium* in the U.K.

While they were filming an interview with me, I was asked about Jesus and God. Now, I know that some subjects are a little taboo for producers to play with, and this was no exception. As soon as the words left the producer's mouth, the black velvet curtain behind me that was being held up by dozens of clamps fell to the ground in one fell swoop. I've never seen a producer skip a question so fast. It was tremendously funny!

What made it even better was that a few weeks later while I was in New York for my book tour, I decided to share the story with Paula Zahn. She asked how could she be sure it was something paranormal if she wasn't there?

A black velvet curtain that looked exactly the same as the one from Sci Fi in London hung behind the camera crew on Paula Zahn's show. The curtain on cue fell to the ground and scared the hell out of the camera crew. My publicist, Ellen, was cracking up. I, on the other hand, had to maintain my composure to answer Paula's very focused questions. Paula was great, by the way, a razor-sharp gal who definitely does her homework, and I really did like her. Out of the many, many interviews that I have done over the last few years, these are the only two where the backdrop curtains fell down. Like I tell Joe, "I didn't do it. Don't look at me, talk to them."

February 8, 2007

I learn about myself and other people every day. On this day I learned of the best as well as the most negative of people. Honestly, you can walk down the street and see both ends of the spectrum any day of the week. I was on a very popular talk show and the topic was, Do you believe? The scenario involved myself, the host, and a qualified research psychologist as well as a skeptic in the audience who described herself as a scientist.

Right before I took the stage, I reflected on the night before when I sat in a booth at the restaurant in my hotel awaiting Joe's arrival. Everything was copacetic until I sensed someone nearby who required my attention. (Joe later referred to this moment as "a disturbance in the force.") My head turned very quickly in the other direction as I focused in on a man across the lobby. I noticed that simultaneously he had also turned sharply toward me. We walked toward each other with no words, and it was then that I realized who he was, and although we had once spoken on the telephone, this was our first time occupying the same space. The man was John Edward, who is also a well-known medium, and it was good finally to cross paths. I invited him and his friend John over to my table, and we did a little medium-to-medium bonding, which was nice.

The producers snapped me back to the current moment as I took the stage following John's interview. I told him he did a great job, hugged him, and traded places with him. I looked into the audience and recognized the faces of the two people whom I had conducted a reading for during the taping of a segment for the television show. I also felt comforted to see the friendly faces of my husband and some of our friends. The taping of the show went great and I loved the majority of the audience, who were open-minded people. There were about six angry women in the back who were the cheering section for the female skeptic on the show, and they were clearly the minority. They could have all been sisters, they were so much alike. Yikes!

I'm going to do my best to articulate to you the situation without throwing in too much of my sarcasm and humor, but sometimes that's hard for me to do, so bear with me. I was trained in a laboratory with real scientists, so this skeptical woman didn't faze me. When she opened her mouth, all I could think of was the Wicked Witch of the West on her bicycle taunting Dorothy who was caught up in a cyclone and trapped in her house. I'm not kidding. I could hear the music from the movie and her saying, "I'll get you, my pretty, and your little dog too!"

Fortunately, I'm well versed in the study of mediumship, having participated for four years in a laboratory, so I'm familiar with laboratory protocol. I felt I shot down her every comment. She was actually set up with a well-known medium for a reading, and we were able to watch the tape of it. The skeptic was impossible. Even people who were on the fence on the subject were rolling their eyes at her negative energy. I was trying to sympathize with her on some small level, but every time I tried she opened her mouth and reminded me that some people just don't get it. Quite honestly, the medium did a great job, given what she had to work with. She got the person who had passed and specific details tied to him, yet all you could hear was a woman demanding basically that her father be resurrected from the dead in order for her to believe that he was there. We're not God.

I told the woman later that she really missed out on a rare opportunity to be read by a talented medium who was actually willing to spend the time fighting her stubborn persona. In addition, I let her know that rather than keeping the medium from connecting with her, she had blocked her father from connecting with her because she had outright denied him. It's sad, but it's the way of the world.

I very much respected Dean Radin, the scientist who was there, who was well versed in the study of the paranormal. I tip my hat to him for his efforts to understand the energy that constructs our souls. I have no problem listening to academics who have no emotional attachment to the study of the paranormal, no chip on their shoulder. I love hearing educated people theorize about what I do. I like to learn from others as much as the next guy. As I watched the female skeptic grow louder and more heated, I must admit it was almost like being in the third grade again watching an eight-year-old lose her cool.

No matter how much published data or scientific studies were pointed out to her, she wouldn't come off her skepticism. We had conducted readings for the show on tape and worked cases, we showed our talent and believed in ourselves, we laid it on the line. My guides once told me in reference to skeptics, "They can't take from you what you have been given." It's true that no one can take your gifts unless you allow it; no matter how hard they try, no one can take from you what they want the most from you. So hold on to your truth and a keen sense of who you are.

Knowing that we had laid it on the line, I had to be comfortable in my own skin, as we all do. My brilliant husband Joe so wisely pointed out that if I asked the skeptic to fill a room with all the people she's helped in life and compare it to the people I've helped, there would be no question of who is living the better life. Joe knows exactly what to say to me to make me feel better. He knows that I am very proud that I've been able to help people to breathe again. It's what keeps me going.

Anyway, it was bothersome to see the people whom I'd read for the show who were sitting in the audience. They were upset with the woman's attitude toward them and their experience. It really causes me to wonder what the payoff is for people like the skeptic. Here is a couple that had lost a loved one less than six months prior, and the skeptic is more worried about being right. I felt good that I was able to make them feel better through my reading, but the skeptic with her negativity had lowered their spirits, and that made me angry. We all have to weigh what is the right or wrong response to someone, especially when dealing with a wounded person. Sometimes life gets going so fast that we shut down emotionally when it comes to empathy for others, and we can become callous and self absorbed. You have to be careful not to let this happen. It eats away at your spirit and can physically take a toll on you and others.

As Joe and I were leaving, I thanked the producers for putting the female skeptic on the show, because she made the rest of us look so good. She could use a few prayers, so when you're thinking about those in need, pray for her. Nobody is beyond enlightenment.

Energy is a powerful thing, and you should pay close attention to the energy you are made of. I've met people who are the center of attention at any gathering because they have great energy and they raise other people's energy. We've all met people whose energy literally drains everybody around them of their own energy and leaves people they come in contact with feeling bad. I think these examples are worth learning from and should cause us to pay attention to our energy and how it affects those around us for better or for worse.

That show will go down in my life as one of my best days ever! What are some of your best days?

I met one of my favorite television icons and spent the day with some of my favorite people. Along the way I made some new friends and I passed the torch, which is really an exciting metaphor for passing on wisdom and positive energy to others, including those from the otherside. I was also able to accomplish this through one of the biggest mediums in the world, TV. I couldn't have asked for more.

Last year required a lot of soul-searching for me. It was challenging and, as usual, my family was my anchor. My kids remind me every day why life is so fantastic, whether it's Fallon telling me that she loves me in opera overtones as she makes it into a song or

Sophia dressing our dog Eleanor up like a police officer or Aurora shooting me a dirty look except she has my eyes and it's strange to have my eyes looking back at me. Fallon sang a song for her teacher's birthday. She selected "Superstition" by Stevie Wonder, and her voice has soul. She was immediately hooked on the applause. Sophia's in gymnastics, bending her little self into a pretzel. Aurora is a cheerleader at her junior high and has discovered boys. Good grief!

I feel like I have more than just those three daughters, though, because the actresses who play my girls are close to my heart too. One of my family's most wonderful memories was in February 2007 with Maria Lark, the charismatic actress who plays Fallon on *Medium*. Maria came to spend the weekend at our house and it was remarkable. She was like family already, so it was a smooth weekend.

We took Maria to Pinnacle Peak Patio for dinner, where my great-grandfather's, grandfather's, dad's, brother's, and now my husband's ties hang from the ceiling. Let me explain. It's a western-themed restaurant, and for more decades than I've been here customers wear an ugly tie in and they call you "city folk" and proceed to cut your tie off and nail it to the ceiling. It's an Arizona tradition. This time I had ties on my four girls—I'm counting Maria. I let them know that they were the first females in our family to hang their ties there, and they roared with laughter.

They thought it was absurd that none of us females had ever worn a tie there before. I took great pictures of Maria and Fallon riding on the mechanical horse, Maria with a black cowboy hat on and Fallon with a suction-cup-tipped bow and arrow. Fallon and Maria bonded and talked about how they're going to live together someday and go to college.

By the time Tuesday rolled around, Maria had to get back home to California. Joe took Maria and her mom, Peggy, to the airport and described to me the process he went through when Maria and Fallon had to be physically separated at the airport with tears flying from their little eyes. Fallon said she'd buy her own airline ticket so that she could stay with Maria in California, and Maria said she wanted to stay in Arizona. They informed Joe and me that when they're grown they're going to live together and have a gum ball machine in their house. It sounds like a good plan to me! We're already making plans to see Maria in California in a couple of weeks when I'm there on business.

It's strange to see Maria and Fallon be so alike, and one plays the other on television. They both hate pink, which I take exception to because I love pink— no, I'm kidding, it's perfectly fine with me. I thought for those of you who watch *Medium* you'd find their story as cute as I did.

Sofia Vassilieva plays Aurora's character on the television show, and she feels like one of my girls too. Recently I met one of the twins who play Sophia on the show. Amanda was so similar looking to Sophia at that age that I wanted to put her in my purse and take her home with us. I didn't realize how attached I'd get to the girls on the show. I have no doubt that they'll always be a part of the DuBois family.

I'm taking my girls to Tokyo in the summer of 2007 while I'm on tour. They're now old enough to travel with us internationally and they really want to eat sushi with their dad, so it should be fun.

I'm content with my decision to return to readings and make more time for short trips with my family. To the girls, I'm just plain "mom," and that's cool with me. I've had the great opportunity to meet people this year from all over the world. I've seen my first book released in Italy, France, Germany, China, Japan, Australia, New Zealand, the U.K., and other countries, and I can't express enough gratitude for the outpouring of affection for my family from people everywhere. I look forward to our girls learning from different cultures and learning various languages and customs. As they get older, I let them come with me a little more when I travel. It is a balancing act. It's hard to tour and "vacation" simultaneously when you work sixteen-hour days going from venue to venue, but it's worth the effort and the girls will have countless terrific memories to look back on. That's what it's all about, right?

My girls all continue to make me proud to be their mom. I'm truly blessed, and I know many parents out there feel just as I do. The good times definitely outweigh the bad, and I've learned many lessons. I think as long as you have the tools to work through the hard times, you'll be fine. Not taking the good times for granted is an important part of getting the most out of life. Sharing your good times with others raises their spirit and encourages them to want much of the same kind of happiness in their own life, so spread the word: live life large, make no apologies for who you are, and love one another. If you do that, you'll never regret your life.

Writing the end of this book is particularly significant to me because it ends my trilogy. Much has changed in my life since I wrote *Don't Kiss Them Goodbye,* which chronicled the loss of my father. I've grown since then, and as fast as life answers my questions, death creates more of them to be answered. My second book, *We Are Their Heaven,* spoke in the voices of people I've read and of their experiences with me and how they've personally coped since losing their beloved to illness, suicide, etc. The purpose of my third installment in this trilogy is to inspire grand living in your life, to change your perspective in a positive way, to share my challenging life experiences with you so that you might relate to how I cope with adversity, and last but not least to let people know that there most definitely is life after death.

Remember to connect with the people who are living, and if you should choose to, use my suggestions to reconnect with the dead. Live two or three lifetimes packed into one life. It's possible to fill many different roles in the world in your lifetime, so don't hold back from who you were born to be and be no less than satisfied with how you've lived. When you look in the mirror, I hope that you really like the person who is looking back. If you don't like what you see, it's never too late to fix it, not as long as you're alive, anyway.

Nothing is quite as gratifying as being a voice that others can relate to, with words that resonate deep down for many so that they can understand and then apply to their own life to live better, fuller lives. I hope that my words strike a chord with you.

My life may have inspired a TV show, but my actual family is very real and unscripted. My girls argue like most siblings do as well as play together. Joe and I have been married for years—I'll just say it's in the teens—and are very much like other married couples with our ups and downs, but the love is always there. Our house is often chaos with a never-ending pile of laundry in the laundry room. The girls like to help me cook, and we make every holiday an event with decorations and sugary treats. When I travel for book tours or press and I'm away from my family, I feel incomplete and can't wait to see them again. I always bring my girls and Joe back little souvenirs from my trips, and the girls knock me over with hugs when I walk through the door, which I love. I have had the rare opportunity to be immortalized through film, but it's my children who truly won't forget me.

Isn't life funny as we stumble through it trying to find the answers to our questions? I was telling Joe how even having done the things that I have, I still find myself critical of death and I attempt to make sense of it, tame it like a wild horse, if you will. I know that eventually I will be trampled by this horse that I call death, but I've found a strange respect for it, as well as a funny bond with it.

I don't fear it. I fight to know it and to teach others to embrace the wisdom that lies in death. Many life lessons can be learned from death. I know that sounds a little strange. What I mean is that if you know that your story will end, then you will make sure that its content is a masterpiece. You'll be certain to not squander your life and to take the time to inspire others through your strength and affection.

Make sure the story of your life is something that you're truly proud of. If it's not, then you have work to do. You want to live a life that's revisited by others, a life that inspires people to be more than they feel they are. Never settle for a life where you simply exist and will be remembered as an underachiever. Living a life that lacks content is a waste of the gifts that you've been given. Anyone can sit back and watch life pass him or her by, but it requires heart to jump in the game and play.

When I start becoming self-absorbed or I'm having a downer day, I try to keep in mind the migration of the monarch butterfly, and I remember that not one of us can make this journey alone. We need each other in order to thrive. I always thought that the monarch seemed to symbolize life because it's so vibrant and free. That thought alone can take away my bad mood and replace it with the realization that one of the most powerful and beautiful words in existence, "life," is a gift that we all have been given to explore and enjoy. So make good use of your gift as I know I'm making good use of mine.

Acknowledgments

$\mathcal{I}$'d like to acknowledge the following people:

My cousin Romaine, who died in 2006, succumbing to cancer after a long battle. I'm proud to be related to such a fun-loving woman, and she is missed. To Pat and Duffy McMahon, who've become like family to Joe and me; you both are dynamic, charismatic people who have changed the world for the better simply by existing. Anyone from Arizona knows who they are and what I mean; words have not been created to describe people like this, but I did my best.

Johnjay Van Es and his beautiful family, and Rich Berra and his: you both give new meaning to "personality," and you have more than your fair share of talent.

Johnjay lost his dad, Big John, this year. I didn't call him Big John because he was a particularly large man but because his presence was big and he was a big man in character and personality. He was so much like my own dad, and everyone who knew him is better off for it. We miss him.

A special mention for little Ryan, who tragically

died far too young at the age of two: you are remembered.

A special mention for the Hartman family: please
know that our hearts go out to you all.

I'd like to thank Mark Gompertz, Ellen Silberman,
Trish Grader, and all the people at Simon & Schuster.
I'm incredibly lucky to work with you all.

And thank you to my readers for sharing what I
have learned through my life experience. I wish you
all the best, and I hope that every one of you finds
your truth in life.

About the Author

ALLISON DUBOIS'S unique story, the inspiration for the hit NBC TV show *Medium*, started during her final semester at Arizona State University, while she was an intern at the district attorney's office. Soon after, researchers at the University of Arizona documented her ability through a series of tests in which she scored exceptionally high on accuracy and specificity. This validation persuaded Allison to become a professional medium and profiler instead of a prosecuting attorney.

In her short career, Allison has conducted more than 2,000 personal readings. In those readings, she helps to ease the pain people feel from losing a loved one. She continues to support the use of science to investigate the afterlife. She spent four years participating in various tests for the University of Arizona.

Allison donates her time to missing and murdered persons and criminal cases for agencies across the country. She is contacted by law enforcement agencies and families to help find missing and murdered people. Allison also assists in jury selection for district attorneys' offices. Each of these is a means for her to give back to the world for being so blessed.

Allison maintains close ties to the show *Medium* as a consultant.

Allison has been featured on *The Today Show, The Big Idea with Donny Deutsch, Last Call with Carson Daly*, and in countless TV shows, magazines and newspapers.